westermann

CAMDEN ROAD

Workbook 5

Erarbeitet von:
Matthew Douglas (St. Catherines, ON, Canada),
Matthias Sitzmann (Schwandorf), Lukas Weidinger (Passau)

Fachliche Beratung:
Sabine Junkers-Haunstetter (Weilheim), Alexander Kulinyak (München),
Petra Ungar (Unterhaching)

Inhaltsverzeichnis

Auf den Seiten zu den einzelnen **Parts** findest du Aufgaben, die deine Englischfähigkeiten trainieren.

Auf den ***Challenge***-Seiten gibt es Aufgaben, die dich herausfordern können.

Mit den ***Check out***-Seiten kannst du weiter üben, wenn dir die *Check out*-Seiten im Textbook noch schwer gefallen sind oder, wenn du noch mehr trainieren möchtest. Im Anhang findest du die Lösungen zu diesen Aufgaben, damit du dich selbst überprüfen kannst.

Damit du die notwendige **Grammatik** immer schnell griffbereit hast, liegt diesem Workbook eine Übersicht (*Grammar in short*) bei, in der alle wichtigen Themen noch einmal kurz und knapp erklärt werden.

Es gibt zusätzlich ein eingelegtes Heftchen mit allen Lösungen.

Im Workbook findest du folgende Verweise:

1 grammar in short	Hier findest du Erklärungen und Beispiele im Grammatik-Einleger.

Dieses Symbol zeigt dir, dass es weiteres Material online gibt. Folgende Materialien sind verfügbar:

2 audio	Audiotrack zur Aufgabe
DIGITAL+ portfolio	Portfolioseiten, auf denen du deine Fortschritte beim Englischlernen sehen kannst
DIGITAL+ wordbank	Vokabelaufgaben zu den Wordbanks im Textbook

Über diesen QR-Code gelangst du auf die Webseite
www.westermann.de/119006
Dort findest du alle Audiotracks und Zusatzmaterialien zum Workbook.

Colour crossword

1a

Do the crossword.

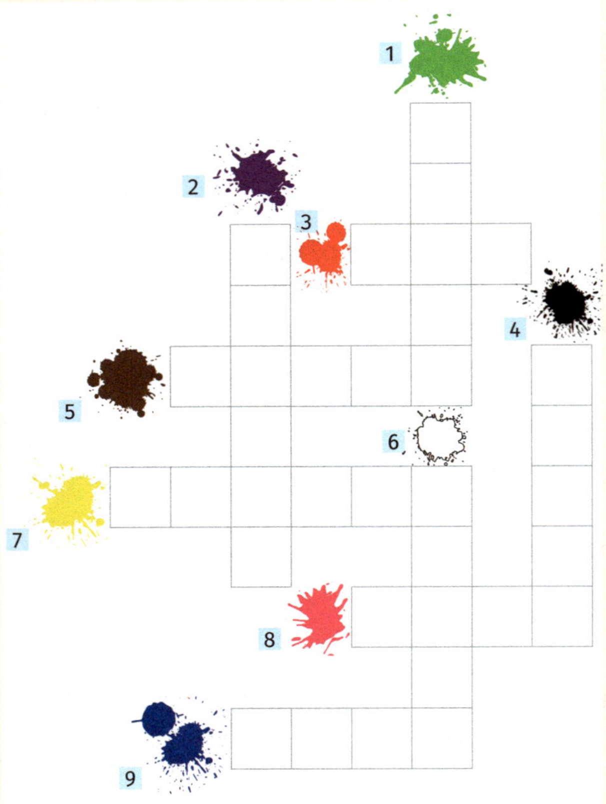

1b

Look at the numbers. Colour the picture.

1 = green | 2 = brown | 3 = orange | 4 = black

Numbers 1-12

2 numbers TB p. 252

Find the numbers.

eight|elevensixthreetwelveonesevenfivetwoninefourten

Hello

3

Write about you.

My name is ______________________________ .

I am ______________________________ years old.

I am from ______________________________ .

My favourite colour is ______________________________ .

So many colours

1

Fill in the missing letters. Then colour in the pencils.

___ la ___ k   ye ___ l ___ w   p ___ n ___   gr ___ ___ n   or ___ ___ ge

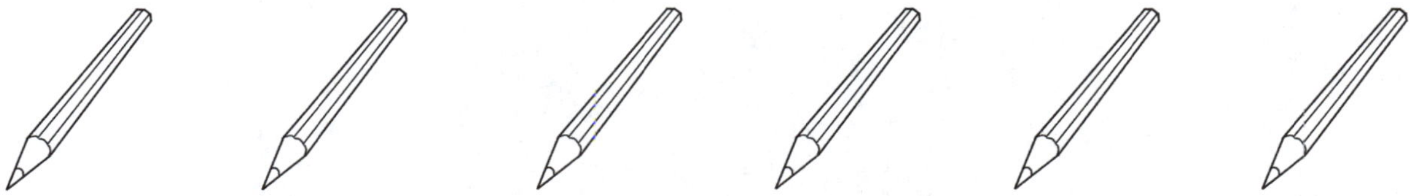

___ ro ___ n   b ___ u ___   w ___ i ___ e   r ___ ___   g ___ e ___   p ___ r ___ le

1, 2, 3, …

2a numbers TB p.252

Write down the numbers as words.

0 zero

1 ___

2 ___

3 ___

4 ___

5 ___

6 ___

7 ___

8 ___

9 ___

10 ___

11 ___

2b audio 1/5

Fill in the missing numbers. Then listen and check your answers.

0 nine | ten | eleven | twelve

1 seven | six | ___ | four | ___

2 three | five | seven | ___ | ___

3 twelve | ___ | eight | six | ___

Farm animals

3a wordbank: animals TB p. 178

Look at the picture. Ask a partner.

cows · horses · pigs · birds · sheep · cats · dogs · rabbits · ...

You can ask:
How many ... are there?

You can answer:
There are ...

3b

Look at the picture again and answer the questions.

0 How many pigs are there? *There are three pigs.*

0 What colour are the pigs? *They are pink.*

1 How many white sheep are there?

2 What colour are the birds?

3 How many light brown cows are there?

4 How many dark brown cows are there?

5 What colour are the cats?

6 What colour are the horses?

7 How many birds are there?

8 How many dogs are there? What colour are they?

9 How many rabbits are there? What colour are they?

The alphabet

4 audio 1/7

Listen and colour the letters. You need seven pencils: red, green, yellow, blue, orange, pink and black.

A B C D E F G

H I J K L M N

O P Q R S T

U V W X Y Z

New in Camden

5a audio 1/10

Listen to Molly and Diego. What does Diego say? Complete the dialogue.

Molly: Hello! My name is Molly. What's your name?

Diego: Hello! My name is Diego.

Molly: Can you spell your name, please?

Diego: *That's* ______

Where ______

Molly: I'm from Leeds. And you?

Diego: ______

______

Molly: I'm eleven years old. And you?

Diego: ______

______

5b

Choose three people in your class. How do you spell their names? Write them down. Then tell a partner.

1 ______

2 ______

3 ______

You can say:

I can spell Sarah. It's S – A – R – A – H.

Tia

1a skill: reading TB p. 166

What is Tia talking about? Read the text and the headings. Write the numbers in the boxes.

1 My family
2 Where I live
3 My pets
4 My favourite activities
5 About me
6 My things
7 My favourite food and drink

[5] Hi, my name is Tia. I'm eleven.

[ ] I've got a brother, Jack. He is thirteen and so cool.

[ ] We're from Camden. That's in London. We live in a small house with our mum and dad.

[ ] I've got a black cat. Her name is Buffy. My brother has got a grey guinea pig and its name is Caspar. They're so cute.

[ ] My favourite food is pizza and my favourite drink is orange juice. And I love sweets.

[ ] I like animals, music and dancing.

[ ] I've got a mobile phone. It is white. And I've got a blue camera. There are lots of photos and posters in my room. Bye.

1b

Read the text again. Find the words.

three words for family members: *brother, …* ____________________

two places: ____________________

two pets: ____________________

a drink: ____________________

three colours: ____________________

two activities: ____________________

Sound check

2 audio 1/13

Listen to the words and sort them into the table. Then say them yourself.

[θ]	[ð]
thing	*the*

~~thing~~ · ~~the~~ · thirteen · this · there · three · Bath · brother

Say it in English

3

Match the German and the English sentences. Write the numbers in the boxes.

1	Wie fragst du jemanden nach seinem Namen?	☐	Where are you from?
2	Wie stellst du dich vor?	☐	What's your name?
3	Wie fragst du jemanden nach seiner Herkunft?	☐	Hi, my name is …
4	Wie fragst du jemanden nach seiner Lieblingsmusik?	☐	What's your favourite music?

Is she …? / Are they …?

4 grammar in short: 1+2 be

Complete the questions and answers with the right forms from the boxes.

1 ________ your cat's name Kitty? — Yes, it is.
2 ________ you eleven years old? — Yes, ________.
3 ________ Jack your father? — No, ________.
4 ________ she your best friend? — Yes, ________.
5 ________ crisps your favourite food? — No, ________.
6 ________ skateboarding and basketball your favourite sports? — Yes, ________.
7 ________ you from Bristol? — No, ________.

Is · Are · Is · Are · Is · Are · Are

I'm not · they are · she is · they aren't · he isn't · I am

Countries

5

Match the English and the German words. Then write the English names of the countries under the flags.

France	Deutschland
Germany	Frankreich
Great Britain	Polen
Poland	Spanien
Turkey	Dänemark
Italy	Großbritannien
Denmark	die Türkei
Spain	Italien

________ ________ France ________

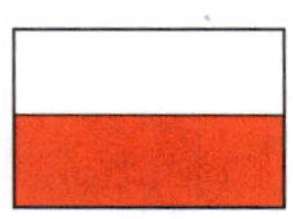

________ ________ ________ ________

Who's she? What's that?

6 grammar in short: 3 personal pronouns

Read the sentences. What do the blue words mean?

0 Tia is eleven. **She** has got a brother. she = Tia

1 Tia's brother is thirteen. **He** is cool. ______

2 Tia and her brother live in a house. **It** is small. ______

3 **They** live in Camden, that's in London. ______

4 Jack has got a guinea pig. **It** is cute. ______

5 Emma is Tia's friend. **She** is from Munich. ______

Sebastian

7 grammar in short: 1 be

Complete the sentences with the long or short forms.

0 I am twelve years old. → I'm twelve years old.

1 You are my best friend. → ______ my best friend.

2 We are from Crewe. → ______ from Crewe.

3 They are nice. → ______ nice.

0 I am a boy. → I'm a boy.

4 ______ my dad. → You're my dad.

5 ______ my sister. → She's my sister.

6 ______ my cats. → They're my cats.

Lena

8 grammar in short: 1 be

Lena has got a message for Ben. Fill in the gaps with the verbs in the negative form.

Hello Ben! My name is Lena. I am eleven. I'm from Poland, I am not (am) from England. I live with my parents in Lublin, but my family ______ (is) from here. We have got a pet called Billy. He ______ (is) a dog, he's a cat. I've got two friends called Toby and Harry. They ______ (are) from Poland, but from Denmark. Their house ______ (is) very big. We ______ (are) in the same class.

What is it?

1a
wordbank: animals TB p. 178

Name the pets.

1 ______
2 ______
3 ______
4 ______
5 ______
6 ______

1b

What do pets eat and drink? Unscramble the words.

1 tuirf: ______
2 blesgeveta: ______
3 terwa: ______
4 cemi: ______
5 god oodf: ______

1c
skill: working with words TB p. 164

Circle the pets blue, the food words black and the adjectives green.

fish · cute · snake · mouse ·
dog food · small · cat · sweet ·
big fruit · dog · dangerous ·
vegetables · guinea pig · friendly

Sneaky

2

Ron talks about Sneaky in school. Write down what he says.

My name is Sneaky.
I am a snake. I am very big.
I am a dangerous pet.
I eat eggs and mice.
I sleep in a cage.
I like the cage.

His name is Sneaky. He is a ______
______
______
______
______
______
______

My pet

3 skill: writing TB p. 167

Look at the word web. Write six sentences about Megan's pet.

carrots — eats — meat

friendly — is — a dog — cute

swims — does tricks — runs fast

the park — likes — Megan

Megan and Ronald

Ronald is Megan's dog and he likes the park.

and · also · or

What do the pets do every day?

4 grammar in short: 4 simple present

Write sentences about the pets.

in water · swims · plays · carrots · watches · in the garden · birds · eats

1 

Sammy

Sammy

2 

Fluffy

3 

Harry

4 

Benji

A homepage

5 grammar in short: 4 simple present

Look at the homepage. Circle the right verb forms.

Pets for adoption

This **am / is** Carla. She **is / are** a cute little cat.
Carla **like / likes** playing with a ball.
She **play / plays** a lot. She **eat / eats** cat food.
She **go / goes** for walks, too.
Carla **sleep / sleeps** in a basket.

This **am / is** our new dog. His name **are / is** Tobi.
He **do tricks / does tricks** and **run / runs** around a lot.
He **is / are** always hungry. We **go / goes** for walks in the park with Tobi. We **give / gives** him dog food.
He **like / likes** vegetables, too.

Ask your classmates

6a

Talk to your classmates. Ask them about their pets or their dream pet. Take notes.

pet's name	animal	is	eats	lives / sleeps in
Rufus	*dog*	*friendly*	*dog food*	*sleeps in a basket*

You can ask:

What's your pet's name?
What animal is it?
How is it?
What does it eat?
Where does it live / sleep?

You can answer:

My pet's name is …
It's a …
It's cute / big / small / …
It eats …
It lives / sleeps in …

6b skill: writing p. 167

Choose one of the pets from 6a. Write 4 sentences about it in your exercise book. Exercise 5 can help you.

An email from a friend

1 skill: mediation TB p. 168

Lies die E-Mail von Sams englischer Freundin Lucy. Hilf Sam dabei, seiner Großmutter zu erklären, was in der E-Mail steht. Bearbeite die Aufgaben stichpunktartig auf Deutsch. Ein Wort genügt nicht.

New Message

To: sam@camdenroad.com

Subject: My new bedroom

Hi Sam!

I have a new bedroom – I'm very happy! My room has got blue walls. On the walls there are posters of my favourite basketball players. There are three shelves. On the shelves there are lots of board games. There is also a desk. This is where I keep my books. Under the desk there is a basket for my cat, Miss Marple. My bed is very big – and it is purple, my favourite colour! It is next to the desk. There's a nice sofa in my room. It is purple, too. I love my new bedroom! What is your bedroom like?

Best wishes, Lucy

Send

1 Welche Farbe haben die Wände?

____

2 Was hängt an den Wänden?

____

3 Wie viele Regale gibt es?

____

4 Wie beschreibt Lucy ihr Bett?

____

5 Was hat Lucy sonst in ihrem neuen Zimmer?

____

____

6 Wie findet Lucy ihr Zimmer?

____

Where is it?

2a

Read the sentences. Draw the missing things in the picture below.

1 There is a football under the bed.
2 There are three books on the shelf.
3 There is a cat next to the sofa.
4 There is a lamp behind the desk.
5 There is a table in front of the sofa.
6 There is a boy in the bed.

2b

Choose two more things and draw them in the picture. Where are they? Write sentences.

1 ______________________________

____

2 ______________________________

____

His or her?

3 grammar in short: 6 possessives

Read the text. Fill in the right *possessive adjectives* from the box. There are more words than you need.

her · she · ~~my~~ · you · our · his · him · Our · they · Their · we · your · our

New Message

To: abdul@camdenroad.com

Subject: My bedroom

Hi, I'm Sophie. I share a bedroom with ___my___ little sister, Claire. ________ bedroom is very small. We have got two beds. My sister has got lots of toys on ________ bed. We have got one desk. There is a cage on the desk for ________ mice. Our mice are called Bubble and Squeak. ________ cage is very big. There is a small sofa next to ________ beds. Our cat, Tom, likes to sleep in our bedroom, too. He thinks the sofa is ________ bed! What have you got in ________ bedroom?

Tom's blue bed

4 audio 1/23, grammar in short: 6 possessives

Listen to the children. What have they got in their bedroom? Write the names.

0  This is ___Tom's___ blue bed.

1  This is ________ purple lamp.

2  This is ________ red ball.

3  This is ________ poster.

4  This is ________ English book.

5  This is ________ guitar.

Family

5 wordbank: people TB p. 179

Match the descriptions and the people.

0 My sister is [E]

1 My grandmother is [ ]

2 My mother is [ ]

3 My brother is [ ]

4 My father is [ ]

5 My grandfather is [ ]

A my mother's father.
B my mother's son.
C my father's mother.
D my grandmother's son.
E my mother's daughter.
F my father's wife.

Megan's family tree

6a audio 1/24, wordbank: people TB p. 179

Listen to Megan. Label the people in Megan's family tree.

Ethan · grandmother · mum · Henry · sister · ~~grandparents~~ · Adam

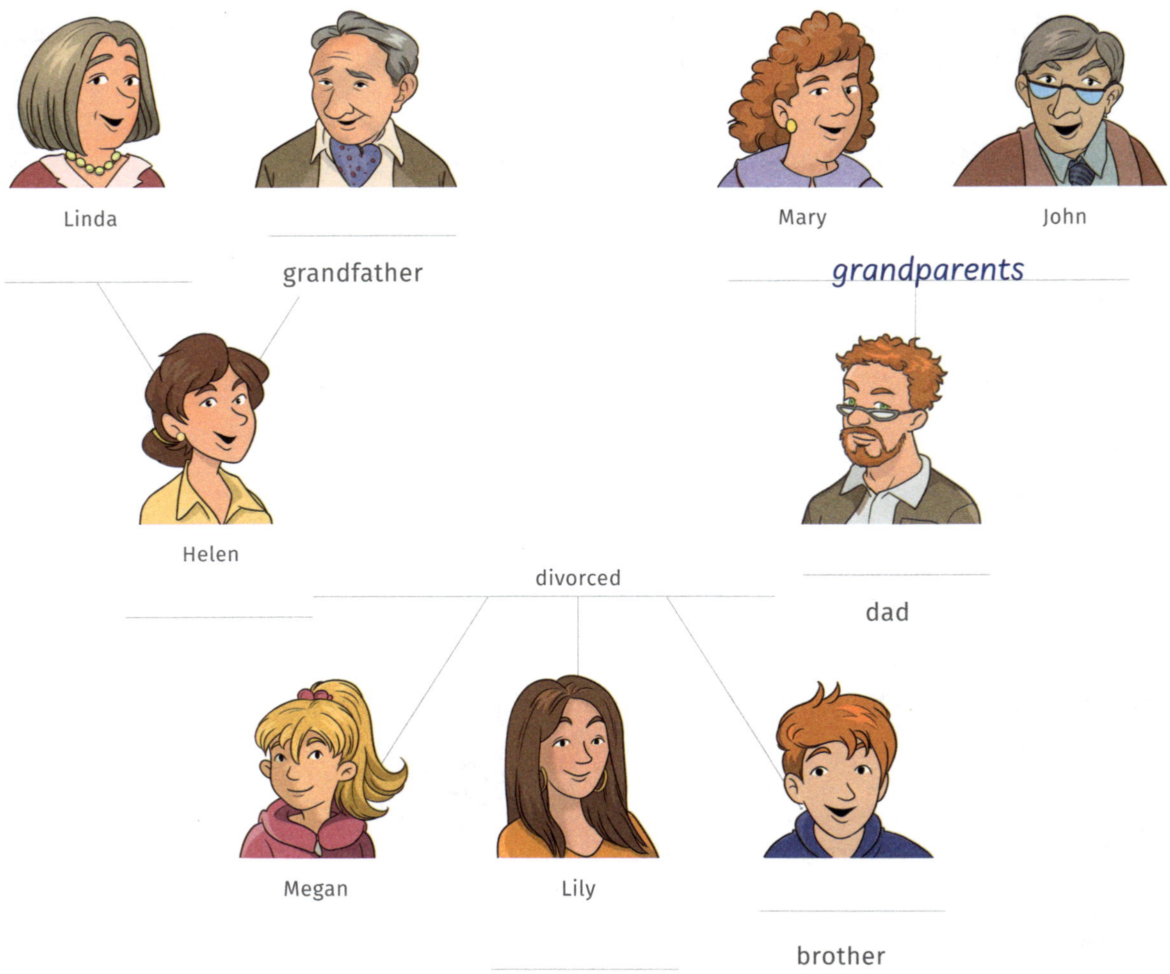

6b

Write six sentences about Megan's family.

Lily is Megan's sister.

Nilufar

1a

Read about Nilufar. Then answer the questions.

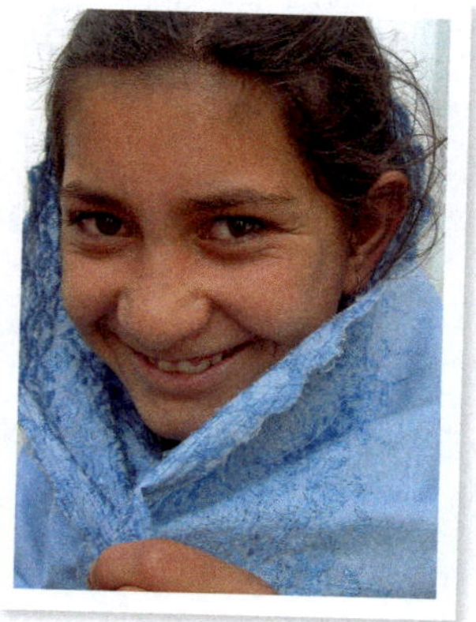

Hi, my name is Nilufar.
I have got brown hair and brown eyes and I am 11 years old.
I live with my family in a big house in Karachi – the biggest city in Pakistan. There are nine people in my family. I have got two brothers, Arash and Meran. They are 7 and 8 years old.
We have also got a cat. His name is Shahzadah and he is brown and white. He likes to play with me and Arash.
My brothers love cricket – and so do I! I like to play cricket with my brothers, but they're small and aren't very good …
Cherries are my favourite food and tea is my favourite drink.
In Pakistan we drink green tea and black tea. I like to drink black tea with lots of sugar.

1 Where does Nilufar live? ______

2 Who does Nilufar live with? ______

3 How old are Nilufar's brothers? ______

4 What does Nilufar's cat like to do? ______

5 What does Nilufar like to eat and drink? ______

1b

Fill in the fact file about Nilufar. Use your answers from 1a to help you.

FACT FILE
Name: Nilufar
Age:
Place:
Hair colour:
Eye colour:
Brothers / Sisters:
Pet:
Likes:
Favourite food:
Favourite drink:

Check out

Speaking solutions p.80

Talk to a partner. Choose a picture and describe the pet. You can use words from the box. Take turns.

1

2

3

4

5

6

fly · run fast · eat fish · play outside · live in water · very small

You can say:

I can see ...
There is / are ...
His favourite ...

Ich kann: über Haustiere sprechen. ◯ sagen, was Tiere (nicht) können. ◯

Writing solutions p.80

Complete the sentences about yourself.

1 My name is ______ .
2 I am ______ years old.
3 I am from ______ .
4 I live in ______ .
5 I like ______ .
6 I don't like ______ .

Ich kann: mich vorstellen. ◯

Mediation solutions p.80

Lies, was Zoe sagt. Beschreibe ihren Bruder stichpunktartig auf Deutsch. Ein Wort genügt nicht.

This is my brother. His name is Zack. He is 13 years old. He lives in London with me and our parents. His favourite colour is red. He has got a red guitar. He loves music.

______
______
______

Ich kann: eine Familie vorstellen. ◯

Reading solutions p.80

Read the sentences and tick (✓) them right, wrong or not in the text.

Hello! My name is Dylan. I am 11 years old. My dream room is big. It has got two beds. One bed is for me and one bed is for my dog, Meg. I have got a computer in my dream room. I have also got a big TV. I watch films at the weekend with my brother.

	✓	✗	---
1 Dylan is 11 years old.			
2 His dream room is small.			
3 It has got one bed.			
4 There is a computer.			
5 He has got a sister.			
6 He plays video games every day.			

Ich kann: eine (Traum-)Zimmerbeschreibung verstehen. ◯

Listening audio 1/28, solutions p. 80

Listen to the interview. Fill in the fact file.

FACT FILE

Name: Jonas

Age:

Place:

Brothers / Sisters:

Pets:

Ich kann: Fragen an eine Person verstehen. ◯

USE OF ENGLISH

Grammar solutions p. 80

Fill in the right *possessive adjectives*.

1 This is ________ cat (I).

2 ________ name is Ginger. (he)

3 Ginger lives in ________ flat. (we)

4 He doesn't like ________ bedroom! (I)

5 This is ________ dog. (my aunt)

6 ________ name is Lola. (she)

7 She sleeps on ________ bed. (my aunt and uncle)

8 She likes to play with ________ shoes! (my uncle)

Vocabulary solutions p. 80

Write down the missing words.

I come from ____________  . I live in a ________ (↔ big) ____________  with my ____________ (*Eltern*). In my room, there is a ________  ________  and a ________  . ________ (↔ under) the ________  , there is a ________  . I have lots of ________  on a shelf. I don't have a ________ (*Fernseher*) in my room, but I have a ________  . What is your home like?

Ich kann: über Haustiere schreiben. ◯ über ein Zuhause sprechen. ◯

Things and people at school

1a wordbank: at school TB p. 181

Find the school words in the snake. Write them down.

teacher|deskpencilcasestudentchairrulerscissorswhiteboardbookpencilpen

teacher, ______________________________

____

____

____

1b

Choose two words from 1a. Write sentences.

____

____

1c

Unscramble these words.

1  hemoowrk ______________

2  serixece koob ______________

3  osloch gba ______________

4  alcdrean ______________

5  ssscoirs ______________

6  licnep esca ______________

More classroom phrases

2 audio 1/34, classroom English TB p. 253

Listen to the classroom scene. Tick (✓) what you hear.

- ☐ Can I open the window, please?
- ☐ Can you open the window, please?
- ☐ No, Joe, it's too warm.
- ☐ No, John, it's too cold.
- ☐ Can you spell it?
- ☐ Can I have your ruler, please?
- ☐ Yes, here you are.
- ☐ You're welcome.
- ☐ Sorry, I can't help.
- ☐ Welcome to Haverstock School, Emma.

Ready for school

3a

Emma is ready for school. What's in her school bag?

In Emma's bag there are scissors, *three books* (book), ______ (folder),

______ (exercise book), ______ (ruler),

______ (rubber),

______ (felt tip),

______ (pen) and

______ (pencil).

3b audio 1/35, numbers TB p.252

Dusty reads the results of his maths homework. Listen to him and write the right numbers.

0 *twenty-seven*

1 ______

2 ______

3 ______

4 ______

5 ______

6 ______

7 ______

Can they do it?

4

Read and answer the questions.

0 Can dogs fly? *No, they can't.*

1 Can babies read? ______

2 Can I drive a car? ______

3 Can dragons make fire? ______

4 Can hamsters swim? ______

5 Can you read this question? ______

Have they got it?

5 grammar in short: 8 have got

Fill in *have got / has got* (✓) or *haven't got / hasn't got* (✗).

1 Tia ________________ (✓) an older brother but she ________________ (✗) a sister.

2 Jack ________________ (✓) many friends.

3 He and his sister Tia ________________ (✓) pets, called Buffy and Caspar.

4 Ben and Tia ________________ (✓) the same class teacher.

5 Ben ________________ (✗) a brother or a sister.

6 Emma and her mother ________________ (✗) a big house in Camden.

Look at him

6 grammar in short: 3 personal pronouns

Fill in the gaps with the right *personal pronouns*.

0 Look at <u>the dragon</u>. Look at ______him______ . He is happy. He likes English lessons.

1 This is Mrs Blum and <u>Emma</u>. Emma's mum helps ________________ find the way to school.

2 Declan has got <u>three brothers and sisters</u> and he loves ________________ .

3 Tia is <u>Jack's</u> sister. Sometimes she goes to the market with ________________ .

4 Emma finds <u>a book</u> with her name in ________________ . <u>She</u> says: "The book is for ________________ ."

A role play

7

Work with a partner. Act out the role play.

Partner A	Partner B
1 Frage, ob es ein Federmäppchen in Bs Schulranzen gibt. "Is there a …?"	2 Sage A, dass du kein Federmäppchen hast. Frage, ob es ein Mäppchen in As Schulranzen gibt. "Is there a …?"
3 Sage B, dass du ein Federmäppchen hast und dass es orange ist.	4 Frage, ob es einen Stift in As Federmäppchen gibt.
5 Sage, dass du keinen Stift hast. Frage, ob B einen hat. "Have you got …?"	6 Sage A, dass du zwei Stifte hast, einen roten und einen blauen.
7 Frage, ob du den blauen haben kannst. "Can I have …?"	8 Sage, dass A ihn haben kann.

A day at Haverstock School

1 audio 1/40, skill: listening TB p. 165

Listen to Rebecca, Archie and Tom and tick (✓) the right answer.

1 Rebecca likes art class on Friday because
- ☐ she likes her teacher.
- ☐ it feels like an early start to the weekend.
- ☐ it's her favourite subject.

2 Archie has maths
- ☐ at 11 o'clock and at 1 o'clock on Tuesday.
- ☐ at 11 o'clock and at 1 o'clock on Thursday.
- ☐ at 10 o'clock and at 2 o'clock on Tuesday.

3 Archie likes
- ☐ maths.
- ☐ science.
- ☐ French.

4 Tom goes to
- ☐ foreign language club.
- ☐ cooking club.
- ☐ drama class.

5 Archie's cooking club is on
- ☐ Monday.
- ☐ Tuesday.
- ☐ Wednesday.

6 Rebecca hopes that she isn't too tired for
- ☐ drama club.
- ☐ her English lesson.
- ☐ robotics club.

1st, 2nd, 3rd, 4th …

2a numbers TB p. 252

Write the ordinal numbers (in words) in the gaps.

0 It's the *first* (1st) time that Emma is in Camden.

1 Her classroom is on the ________ (3rd) floor.

2 Tia's cat Buffy was born on the ________ (11th) of June.

3 June is the ________ (6th) month of the year.

4 Friday is the ________ (5th) day of the week.

5 February is the ________ (2nd) month of the year.

6 Tia's birthday is on ________ (22nd) April.

7 The ________ (4th) day of the week is Thursday.

8 Today is the ________ (?) of ________ (month).

2b

You run in a race and pass the person in 2nd place. What position are you in?

You are in ________ place.

So many clocks

3a wordbank: time TB p. 182

Draw the hands on the clocks. Write the time on the digital clocks.

four o'clock

half past one / one thirty

quarter past seven / seven fifteen

quarter to eight / seven forty-five

quarter past ten

twelve o'clock

3b

Write down the times in words.

My Mondays

4 wordbank: time TB p. 182

Look at the pictures. When do you do these things? Write down the times and draw the clock hands.

I get up at

I clean my teeth at

I go to school at

I come home from school at

I start my homework at

I go to bed at

My timetable

5a wordbank: at school TB p. 181

Write your timetable. Look at the box for the subjects.

art · biology · drama · English · French · German · geography · history · ICT · maths · music · PE · RE · science · D&T

Monday	Tuesday	Wednesday	Thursday	Friday

5b

Answer the questions.

1 On what days are your English lessons at school? ______

2 How many German lessons do you have every week? ______

3 Who is your English teacher? ______

4 What's your favourite subject? ______

5 What's your favourite day of the week? ______

They don't …

6 grammar in short: 4 simple present

Complete the sentences. Use the negative form *doesn't* or *don't* (✗) and the verb in brackets.

0 Tia, Declan, Jack and Ben *don't meet* (✗ meet) in front of the school.

1 The students ______ (✗ want) to be late for registration.

2 Ben ______ (✗ forget) his maths homework.

3 Emma and Tia ______ (✗ like) their school uniform.

4 Jack ______ (✗ sleep) enough.

5 Emma is very good at basketball but she ______ (✗ like) hockey.

How to get to school

1

Find translations for the words and fill in the crossword puzzle.

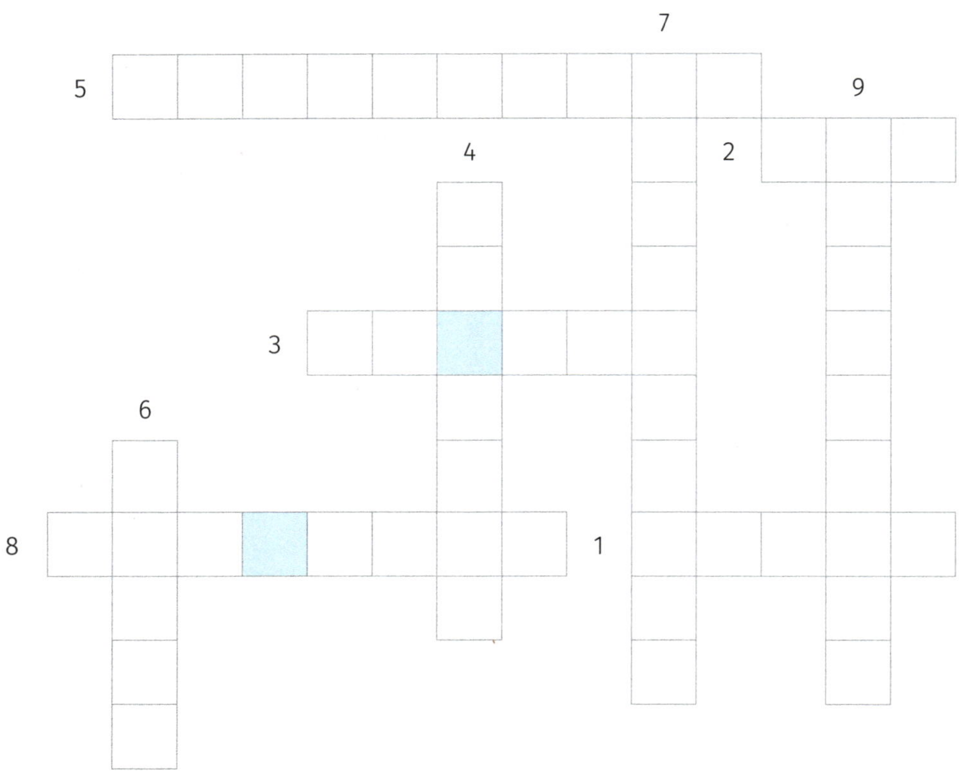

1 Zug
2 Auto
3 mit dem Bus
4 zu Fuß
5 Name von Emmas Schule
6 beeilen
7 Klassenkameraden
8 Bushaltestelle
9 sich entschuldigen

The breakfast table

2 wordbank: food and drink TB p. 184

Can you write these words in English? Find them in the wordsearch.

0 Messer knife
1 Löffel ______
2 Gabel ______
3 Teller ______
4 Tee ______
5 Milch ______
6 Saft ______
7 Toast ______
8 Konfitüre ______

t	a	i	e	s	t	l	n	z	r
e	b	e	x	p	l	a	t	e	a
a	l	t	p	o	l	i	w	o	s
w	e	s	e	o	i	g	t	k	a
i	d	f	n	n	k	a	z	n	f
q	t	g	s	e	e	j	h	i	e
f	o	r	k	u	i	u	t	f	a
i	a	f	n	r	k	i	z	e	j
h	s	m	i	l	k	c	d	o	a
s	t	v	b	w	m	e	p	i	m

What do they like?

3a grammar in short: 4 simple present, wordbank: food and drink TB p. 184

The friends don't eat everything. Write down what they like and what they don't like.

1 Emma and Jack (✗ like)  ______________________

2 Tia (✓ like)  ______________________

3 Ben (✗ eat)  ______________________

4 Declan (✓ drink)  ______________________

5 The Hendersons (✗ eat)  ______________________

6 Ben (✓ love)  ______________________

3b grammar in short: 4+5 simple present

What do the friends do? Unscramble the questions and write the answers.

0 friends – ? – Jack – Does – lots of – have

Does Jack have lots of friends? — *Yes, Jack has lots of friends.*

1 rugby – Emma – Does – ? – play

______________________ ______________________

2 ? – do – meet – Where – the pupils

______________________ ______________________

3 Does – tea – ? – like – Tia – to drink

______________________ ______________________

4 ? – like – Do – Ben and Declan – fruit

______________________ ______________________

Snow day? No way!

4 skill: mediation TB p. 168

Lies die Texte und beantworte die Fragen stichpunktartig auf Deutsch. Ein Wort genügt nicht.

Hello, I'm Sophie from Manchester. Today is a great day – I don't have school! When it snows a lot in the UK, students and teachers can't get to school because we can't ride our bikes and the buses stop. A lot of schools are not open and we have a 'snow day'. Some schools have lessons online when it snows, but not at my school – no lessons, no homework, just fun in the snow all day!

Hi, I'm Jake. I live on Mackinac Island. That's in Michigan, in the USA. Most of the students at my school live very close to school and use a snowmobile to get to school in winter. For students and teachers here, it is normal to go to school on a snowmobile. And it's fun, too! We can only do it from November to April, then we have to walk or go by bike. Winter is my favourite time of year. But there are no snow days for us!

1 Was ist ein *snow day*?

2 Wie verbringt Sophie ihren *snow day*?

3 Wie kommen Schülerinnen und Schüler auf Mackinac Island im Winter zur Schule?

4 Wann liegt Schnee auf Mackinac Island?

5 Wie kommt man in den Sommermonaten zur Schule?

Sound check

5 audio 1/46

Listen to the words and sort them into the table. Then say them yourself.

[/v/]	[/w/]	[/r/]
have	*want*	*room*

~~room~~ · ~~have~~ · ~~want~~ · read · way · weekend · love · right · live · red · walk · every · wall · window · interactive · brother · give · write · what · video · hurry

School expert

1a classroom English TB p. 253

Unscramble the classroom phrases.

0 quiet! – be

Be quiet!

1 can I – the toilet? – go to

2 which – on? – page – are we

3 open the window – please? – can you

4 "Federmäppchen" – what's – in English?

5 exercise. – can't – I – understand – this

1b numbers TB p. 252

Let's do some Maths. Fill in the gaps. Write the numbers in words.

1 *thirteen* plus ______ minus ______ is ______
13 + 19 – 7 = ???

2 ______ minus ______ plus ______ is ______
11 – 3 + 15 = ???

3 ______ plus ______ minus ______ is ______
18 + 14 – ??? = 19

1c wordbank: time TB p. 182

Read the text. Then think: It is 8.30 a.m. in London. What time is it in the cities around the world?

WORLD TIME

It's not the same time everywhere in the world. For example, when it is 12 o'clock (lunchtime) in England, it is 1 o'clock in the afternoon in Germany. The USA and Australia have different time zones. In New York, it's 6 o'clock in the morning and in Sydney it's 8 o'clock in the evening, when it's lunchtime in England. In India it's half past three in the afternoon at the same time. Of course one time zone can be for more than one country. England and Ireland are in the same time zone, for example.

0 Munich

9.30 a.m.

1 New York

2 New Delhi

3 Sydney

4 Dublin

5 Washington D.C.

Check out

Speaking solutions p.81

Get together with a partner. Your partner opens the workbook at page 25. Ask each other questions about your school timetable. Take turns.

You can ask:

What do we have on Monday mornings?
When do we have ... ?
What is your favourite day?

You can answer:

We have maths and then history.
We have ... on Thursday afternoons at 2pm.

Ich kann: über Stundenpläne und Schulfächer sprechen. ◯

Listening audio 1/51, solutions p.81

Listen to Olivia. Write short answers to the questions (1-5).

1 How many lessons does Olivia have every day?

____

2 What is her favourite subject?

____

3 Why doesn't she like Monday mornings?

____

4 What does she have on Wednesday afternoons?

____

5 What does Mrs Faith teach?

____

Ich kann: einen Hörtext über Schule und Klasse verstehen. ◯

Reading solutions p.81

Read the sentences and tick (✓) them right, wrong or not in the text.

Hi! I'm Sam. Every morning, I have my breakfast with my sister, Jasmin. In the week, we always eat cereal. I usually drink orange juice, but my sister likes to drink milk. Sometimes I also eat an apple if I am really hungry. On Sundays, we don't eat cereal. We have a warm breakfast, like toast, eggs and sausages. I love Sundays!

	✓	✗	---
1 Jasmin is Sam's sister.			
2 They eat different breakfasts.			
3 Sam usually drinks milk.			
4 Sometimes Sam eats an apple, too.			
5 Sam eats cereal every day.			
6 He plays video games every day.			
7 Jasmin loves Sundays.			

Ich kann: einen Text über Frühstücksgewohnheiten verstehen. ◯

Writing solutions p.81

Complete the sentences about your school*.

**Realschule*: secondary school

1 The name of my school is ______________________________ .

2 Lessons start at ____________ and they end at ____________ .

3 We have a break from ____________ until ____________ .

4 My favourite subject is ____________ because ____________ .

5 I have it on ____________ at ____________ .

Ich kann: meine Schule und Klasse beschreiben. ◯ Uhrzeiten nennen. ◯

Mediation solutions p. 81

Lies, was die Lehrkraft sagt. Bearbeite die Aufgaben stichpunktartig auf Deutsch. Ein Wort genügt nicht.

Please listen, everyone. For the maths test tomorrow, you need a black pen. Please do not use a blue pen. You also need a pencil and a ruler. A rubber is a good idea, too. But you don't need paper. The test starts at 10 o'clock tomorrow morning, so please don't be late!

1 Was steht morgen an?

______

2 Was braucht man?

______

3 Was braucht man nicht?

______

4 Was soll man nicht verwenden?

______

5 Wann geht es los?

______

6 Worauf sollen die Schüler achten?

______

Ich kann: eine Aussage über Schulsachen verstehen. ◯

USE OF ENGLISH

Grammar solutions p. 81

Read the sentences and write down the negatives.

0 Tom drinks orange juice. *Tom doesn't drink orange juice.*

1 Mrs Newton teaches science. ______

2 We have got ten books. ______

3 Our school is in France. ______

4 I read a book every day. ______

5 He can play football. ______

6 They like maths. ______

Vocabulary solutions p. 81

Write down the missing words.

On Saturdays, I always have a ______  and two ______  . I like to have some ______  and ______  , too. I don't like ______  . To drink, I have ______  with some ______ 

. I also have a glass of ______  .

Ich kann: Sätze im *simple present* verneinen. ◯ über Frühstücksgewohnheiten sprechen. ◯

Family, friends and festivals

1a grammar in short: 6 possessives

Whose present is it? Write it down.

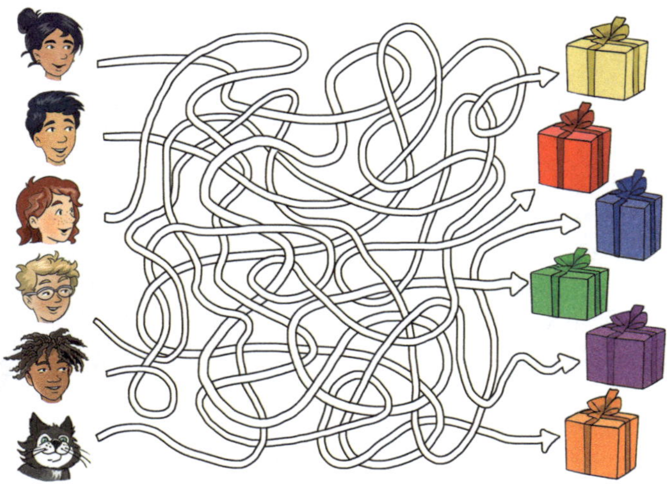

0 *Buffy's present is* ________ red.

1 ________ green.

2 ________ blue.

3 ________ yellow.

4 ________ orange.

5 ________ purple.

1b

Do you remember the festivals? Who likes them? Fill in the gaps.

0 Mrs Jordan

Mrs Jordan's favourite festival is *Christmas* .

1 the Chopras

________ favourite festival is ________ .

2 Nele

________ favourite festival is ________ .

3 Tina

________ favourite festival is ________ .

4 the Woodins

________ favourite festival is ________ .

5 the children

________ favourite festival is ________ .

1c

Look at the photos in 1b again. Match the sentences and the photos. There is one sentence too many.

- [ ] Trick or treat?
- [ ] Now it is here – Happy New Year!
- [ ] Happy birthday to you!
- [ ] Happy Pancake Day!
- [ ] Merry Christmas!
- [ ] Roses are red, violets are blue, sugar is sweet, and so are you.

Christmas tongue twisters

2

Read aloud.

1 Rudi reindeer runs round red wreaths.
2 Pretty presents perfectly packed in paper.
3 Seven Santas sang silly songs.
4 Santa's sleigh slides on slick snow.

Kaan's presentation about Eid

3 skill: mediation TB p. 168

Kaan stellt sein Lieblingsfest vor. Lies den Text und fülle das *fact file* stichpunktartig aus.

My favourite festival is Eid. It's a three-day festival when Muslims around the world celebrate the end of Ramadan. It's one of the most important holidays in Islam and it happens at a different time every year. In Turkey, Eid, or "Bayram", is a really big festival. We wear our best clothes and go to the mosque. Then we visit our grandparents – Grandma makes the best baklava! Children visit the neighbours and say "Eid Mubarak!" to everyone.

Meine Freunde feiern Feste
Thema:
Präsentation von:
Informationen zum Fest
Religion:
Dauer:
Wann:
Anlass:
Wie man feiert:
Glückwunsch

What's going on?

4a grammar in short: 9 present progressive, skill: describing pictures TB p. 172

Look at the picture. Tell a partner what the people are doing.

buy · eat · look at · stand · point at · talk · walk · dance · play

4b

Look at the picture again. What are the people wearing? Write eight sentences.

Text message

1 skill: mediation TB p. 168

Schaue dir den Chat zwischen Tia und ihrer Mutter an. Bearbeite die Aufgaben stichpunktartig auf Deutsch. Ein Wort genügt nicht.

1 Warum schreibt Tia ihrer Mutter?

2 Warum möchte die Mutter wissen, ob Tias Opa kommt?

3 Warum fragt Tia nicht selbst?

4 Wie soll Tia an die Nummer kommen?

5 Warum geht das nicht?

6 Warum erledigt sich das Problem von selbst?

Tia Hi Mum are Grandma and Grandpa coming to my party today?

Mum I don't know. I'm on my way to the supermarket. Can you ask them? We need lots of burgers for Grandpa, then. He loves burgers!

Tia Sorry, I haven't got their mobile number.

Mum Oh, Tia, ask Dad! He has got the number. Are you meeting me at the supermarket?

Tia Sorry, Dad isn't home. Yes, I'm leaving now.

Mum Just a second. My phone is ringing. It's Grandma! 😉

Pounds and pence

2 wordbank: shopping and money TB p. 178

You have £10. Write down the change you get when you buy these things.

0  £2.50 — *£8.50 – eight pounds fifty*

1  £1.00

2  £3.75

3  £4.45

4  £2.25

5  £0.99

6  £3.25

7  £1.35

A maths lesson

3 numbers TB p. 252

Complete the crossword. Write down the numbers in words.

ACROSS →

3 ninety-two minus fifty-two
5 seventeen plus thirty-three
6 thirteen plus seven
7 one hundred minus ten
10 twenty-five plus fifty-five
11 seventy-six minus sixty-four
12 forty-six minus forty-one
14 one hundred minus eighty-nine

DOWN ↓

1 fourteen plus forty-six
2 seven plus eight
4 ninety-nine minus sixty-nine
8 thirty-five minus seventeen
9 eighty-eight minus eighty-five
13 forty plus thirty

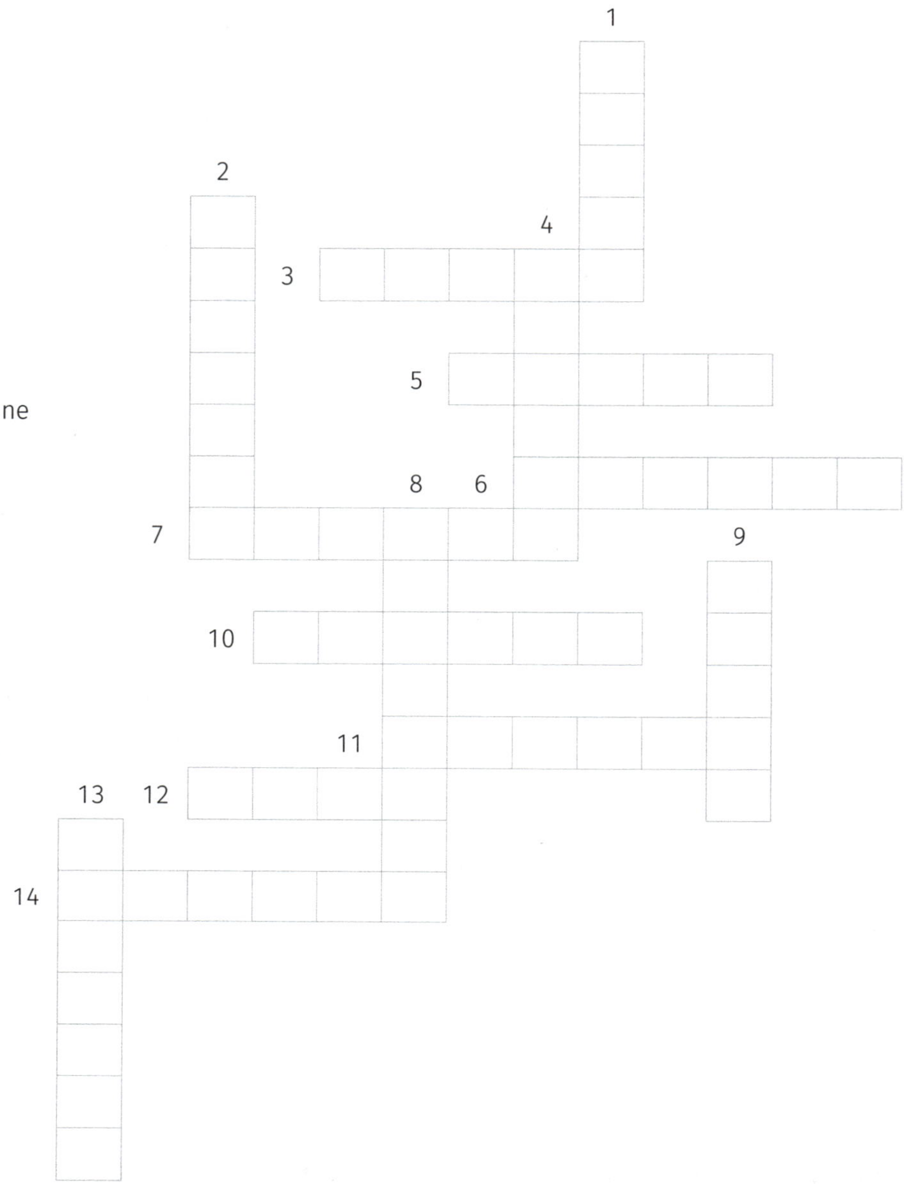

Sound check

4 audio 1/62

Listen to the words and sort them into the table. Then say them yourself.

[æ]	[eɪ]
hat	*cake*

~~hat~~ · ~~cake~~ · carrot · sandwich · paper · Friday · fantastic · plan · game · lemonade

The day after the party

5a grammar in short: 9+10 present progressive

Look at the pictures. Ask questions and give answers.

0

Tom / play / tennis

0

John / Ellie / go / school

1

Rosie / ride / horse

2

parents / work / house

3

Tom / sing / song

4

Sophie / use / computer

5

family / have / breakfast

6

Zoe / walk / the dog

0 *Is Tom playing tennis? – No, he isn't. He's playing football.*

0 *Are John and Ellie going to school? – Yes, they are.*

1 ______

2 ______

3 ______

4 ______

5 ______

6 ______

5b

Work with a partner. Look at the picture and choose a person. Answer your partner's questions.

Partner A can ask:

Is the person reading a book?
Is he / she playing with the dog?

Partner B can answer:

No, they aren't. / Yes, they are.
No, he / she isn't. / Yes, he / she is.

At Tia's party

1 grammar in short: 9 present progressive

Read the text on page 66 in your textbook again. Fill in the gaps.

0 Tia and her dad _are preparing_ the barbecue.

1 Tia ________________ from the shelves.

2 She ________________________ and forks into the garden.

3 Buffy ________________ with a balloon.

4 Tia's friends ________________________ presents.

5 The friends ________________ burgers.

6 Tia ________________ her presents.

7 Buffy ________________ the mice on the box.

8 Tia's dad ________________ photos.

Find the one

2a numbers TB p. 252

Find the right person.

1 2 3 4 5

0 The skirt of the _seventh_ person is blue.

1 The shorts of the ________________ person are green.

2 The socks of the ________________ person are red.

3 The trousers of the ________________ person are blue.

4 The scarf of the ________________ person is red and green.

5 The skirt of the ________________ person is red.

6 The skirt of the ________________ person is blue.

7 The dress of the ________________ person is pink.

6 7

2b

Find the odd one out.

0  0 *the fifth cake*

1  1 ______

2  2 ______

3  3 ______

4  4 ______

5  5 ______

6  6 ______

Difficult words

3 grammar in short: 11 plural forms

Do you remember the words? Write down the right forms.

0  one *mouse* → two *mice* 

1  one ______ → two ______ 

2  one ______ → two ______ 

3  one ______ → two ______ 

4  one ______ → two ______ 

5 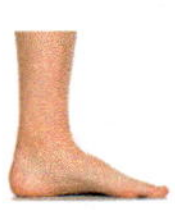 one ______ → two ______ 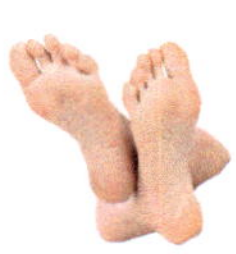

6  one ______ → two ______ 

7  one ______ → two ______ 

Tia's birthday muffins

4a grammar in short: 8 have got

Tia wants to make muffins for her birthday. Read the list and look at the picture. Talk to a partner. What has Tia got and what hasn't she got?

Dear Tia,
For the muffins you need:
- *250 g flour*
- *120 g sugar*
- *120 g butter*
- *200 g milk*
- *2 large eggs*
- *100 g dark chocolate*

You'll also need a big bowl, a muffin tin and a spoon.
Love, Mum

You can say:
Tia's got …
Yes, but she hasn't got …

4b

Now read the recipe for the muffins. Match the English sentences and the German translations.

1 Heat the oven to 180°C. ______
2 Put the flour, sugar, butter, milk and eggs into a large bowl. ______
3 Mix everything together with a big spoon. ______
4 Cut the chocolate into small pieces. ______
5 Put the chocolate in the bowl and mix again. ______
6 Put everything into a muffin tin. ______
7 Put the tin in the oven and bake for 20 minutes. ______

A Gib Schokolade in die Schüssel und rühre weiter.
B Gib die Form in den Ofen. Die Backzeit beträgt 20 Minuten.
C Gib Mehl, Zucker, Butter, Milch und Eier in eine große Schüssel.
D Fülle alles in eine Muffinform.
E Schneide die Schokolade in kleine Stücke.
F Verrühre alles mit einem großen Löffel.
G Heize den Ofen auf 180 Grad vor.

4c skill: presentations TB p. 170

Now it's your turn. Buy all the things you need and bake your own muffins. Bring them to school. Or you can make a video of how you make your muffins. Present it to your class and tell them about it.

There's something wrong

1 grammar in short: 9+10 present progressive

Write questions and give right answers. Use the *present progressive*.

0 mum / wear / cap *Is the mum wearing a cap? – No, she isn't. She's wearing a party hat.*

1 girls / dance

2 cat / play / with a ball

3 mum / carry / a balloon

4 dad / eat / a hot dog

5 boys / play / football

6 the dog / wear / a red hat

7 parents / sleep / on the sofa

8 the dog / play / cards

Check out

Speaking solutions p. 82

Talk to a partner. Ask and answer questions. Take turns.

0 
Zoe 6 / 10

1 
Mike 15 / 7

2 
Yusra 23 / 2

3 
Moe 1 / 1

4 
Val 2 / 5

5 
Walt 17 / 9

You can ask:
When is Zoe's birthday?

You can answer:
Zoe's birthday is on the sixth of October.

Ich kann: sagen, wann jemand Geburtstag hat. ◯

Mediation solutions p. 82

Schaue dir das Poster an. Bearbeite die Aufgaben stichpunktartig auf Deutsch. Ein Wort genügt nicht.

1 Wann und wo findet die Party statt?

2 Wer ist eingeladen?

3 Wieviel kostet der Eintritt?

4 Was gibt es zu essen? (Nenne 3 Dinge.)

Ich kann: ein Poster über ein internationales Fest verstehen. ◯

Reading solutions p. 82

Read the sentences and tick (✓) them right, wrong or not in the text.

Robin Hi Alice! I am having a great birthday party. All my friends are here and we are having lots of fun. My little brother is eating lots of chocolate. My mum is playing games with my aunt and uncle. I think my mum is winning. My friends and I are dancing a lot. Oh, my grandma is bringing a cake into the living room and now everybody is singing! What a perfect party!

	✓	✗	---
1 Robin is celebrating her birthday.			
2 Her brother is eating lots of crisps.			
3 Her aunt and uncle are playing games.			
4 Robin is dancing with her friends.			
5 Robin's grandpa is at the party, too.			

Ich kann: verstehen, was gerade passiert. ◯

Writing solutions p. 82

Write about your perfect meal. Write 30 words or more.

You can write:

For my perfect meal, I eat … ______ *I drink …* ______

For dessert, I have … ______

______

______

______

______

______

Ich kann: über Essen und Getränke schreiben. ◯

Listening audio 2/8, solutions p. 82

Listen. Find the right order of the pictures. Be careful, there are more pictures than you need.

Ich kann: verstehen, was jemand gerade tut. ◯

USE OF ENGLISH

Grammar solutions p. 82

a) What is Chloe doing? Write down short answers.

0 Is she doing her homework? ✓ *Yes, she is.*

1 Is she sitting outside? ✗ ______

2 Is she listening to music? ✓ ______

3 Is she eating her dinner? ✗ ______

4 Are she and her sister dancing? ✗ ______

b) Use the right form of the verbs in the box.

do · write · read · drink

1 Amelia ______ a book.

2 Benjamin ______ a cup of tea.

3 Mr Thomas ______ a text message.

4 I ______ this task.

Vocabulary solutions p. 82

Underline the wrong word and think of a suitable word for each line.

0 We are <u>swimming</u> a present for our dad. *buying*

1 It his Monday tomorrow. ______

2 Oh, I like the socks. They are very bad. ______

3 They're great! When much are they? ______

4 They are just 10 pancakes. ______

Ich kann: sagen, was gerade passiert. ◯ Einkaufsvokabeln verwenden. ◯

Blind football

1 skill: mediation TB p. 168

Lies den Text über Blindenfußball und korrigiere die Fehler in den fünf Sätzen auf Deutsch.

Andy from London is blind. He is 13 years old and his favourite hobby is football. There are five players in each team, four blind players and a goalkeeper. The goalkeeper can see. The football makes a noise when it moves so that the players know where it is. The goalkeepers tell their players where they have to run. There is another person behind each goal who tells the players where the goal is and when they can shoot. And the players talk to their teammates, so the fans have to be really quiet. These rules are important for blind people playing football. Andy loves his sport and he says that he can see with his ears.

1 Andy und seine Teammitglieder sind alle blind.

2 Der Fußball macht kein Geräusch, damit die Spieler nicht abgelenkt werden.

3 Der Torwart sagt den Spielern, wo das Tor liegt.

4 Die Person hinter dem Tor sagt den Spielern, wo sie hinlaufen sollen.

5 Während des Spiels feuern die Fans ihr Team lautstark an.

Word snake

2 wordbank: free time TB p. 188

Find eight hobby words in the snake. Write them down.

dancing|tabletennisridingkaratetravellingcomputergamesclimbinginlineskating

dancing

1 DAS VERB BE: AUSSAGEN

the verb be: statements TB p. 144

Wenn du über Personen, Tiere oder Dinge sprechen willst, kannst du die Formen *am*, *is* und *are* benutzen. Sie sind Formen des Verbs *be*. Im gesprochenen Englisch werden sie oft verkürzt.

I am Emma. → I'm Emma.
She is twelve. → She's twelve.
We are from Camden. → We're from Camden.

Die Formen von *be* kannst du verneinen, indem du *not* einfügst. Auch hier gibt es Lang- und Kurzformen.

I am not Emma. → I'm not Emma.
She is not twelve. → She isn't twelve.
We are not from Camden. → We aren't from Camden.

2 DAS VERB BE: FRAGEN

the verb be: questions TB p. 145

Entscheidungsfragen sind Fragen, die man mit „Ja“ oder „Nein“ beantworten kann. Wenn du die Entscheidungsfrage mit einer Form von *be* stellen willst, stellst du diese an den Satzanfang. Man antwortet darauf meist mit einer Kurzantwort.

Am I in your team?	Yes, you are.	No, you aren't.
Are you eleven?	Yes, I am.	No, I'm not.
Is he/she/it twelve?	Yes, he/she/it is.	No, he/she/it isn't.
Are they from London?	Yes, they are.	No, they aren't.

Wenn du eine Frage mit Fragewort stellen willst, stellst du das Fragewort an den Anfang. Auch hier werden in gesprochener Sprache häufig Kurzformen verwendet.

What is your name? → **What**'s your name?
Where is your friend from? → **Where**'s your friend from?
Who is that? → **Who**'s that?

Dustys Hinweis

Achtung: ***who*** (Wer?) und ***where*** (Wo?) verwechselt man leicht!

3 PERSONALPRONOMEN

personal pronouns TB p. 146

Anstatt ein Nomen mehrmals zu verwenden, kannst du es durch ein Personalpronomen ersetzen, wenn klar ist, worauf es sich bezieht. Es kann sowohl das Subjekt (*wer* oder *was*?) als auch ein Objekt (*wen* oder *was*?) ersetzen.

I want to draw a picture.	Can you give me a pen, please?
You are new in class.	Tia can show you the school.
He needs help.	Can you help him?
She's my friend.	I like her.
This is my bike. It's new.	Do you like it?
We want to play football.	You can come with us.
Where are you?	I can't find you.
They are in the garden.	I can see them.

4 DIE EINFACHE GEGENWART: AUSSAGEN

the simple present: statements TB p. 147

Wenn du ausdrücken willst, dass jemand etwas regelmäßig tut oder dass etwas regelmäßig stattfindet, verwendest du das *simple present*. In der 3. Person Singular *(he, she, it)* hängst du ein -s an. Signalwörter für die Verwendung des *simple present* sind zum Beispiel *always, often, never, every day, on Mondays und in the morning.*

I meet my friends on Fridays.	The dance club meets on Fridays.
You like the science club.	Tia likes the science club.
We need a green folder for Maths.	Emma needs a green folder for Maths.
They eat apples, salad and carrots.	The guinea pig eats apples, salad and carrots.

Für die Verneinung fügst du *don't (do not)* bzw. bei der 3. Person Singular *doesn't (does not)* ein.

I don't play football.	He/She/It doesn't play football.
You don't play football.	
We don't play football.	
They don't play football.	

5 DIE EINFACHE GEGENWART: FRAGEN

the simple present: questions TB p. 148

Bei Entscheidungsfragen im *simple present* stellst du ein *do* oder *does* an den Satzanfang. Bei der 3. Person Singular hat das Hauptverb dann kein -s. In den Kurzantworten wird *do* oder *does* aufgegriffen.

Do I worry too much?	Yes, you do.	No, you don't.
Do you like tea?	Yes, I do.	No, I don't.
Does he/she/it eat toast?	Yes, he/she/it does.	No, he/she/it doesn't.
Do they go to Haverstock School?	Yes, they do.	No, they don't.

Bei Fragen mit Fragewort steht das Fragewort am Satzanfang vor *do* oder *does*.

What do you think about your new school?
When does school start?

6 BESITZVERHÄLTNISSE AUSDRÜCKEN

possessives TB p. 149

Wenn du sagen möchtest, wem oder zu wem etwas gehört, hast du im Englischen verschiedene Möglichkeiten.
Du kannst es z. B. mithilfe des s-Genitivs ausdrücken.

Im Singular hängst du an das Nomen einen Apostroph und ein s an: 's	Bei regelmäßigen Pluralformen fügst du nur den Apostroph an das Plural -s an.	Bei unregelmäßigen Pluralformen, die nicht auf -s enden, hängst du ein 's an.
Emma's room	the parents' bikes	the children's room

Wenn du sagen willst, dass etwas zu einer Sache gehört, kannst du eine Konstruktion mit *of* verwenden:
The name of the school is Haverstock School.

Possessivbegleiter sind Wörter, die man statt eines Nomens mit s-Genitiv verwenden kann:
Emma's lives in Camden. Her room is big. (statt: Emma's room is big.)

My house is big.	Our house is big.
Your house is big.	Your house is big.
His/Her/Its house is big.	Their house is big.

Dustys Hinweis
Im Deutschen verwendet man beim Genitiv-s keinen Apostroph!

7 DER ARTIKEL

the article TB p. 150

Anders als im Deutschen gibt es im Englischen nur eine Form des bestimmten Artikels: *the*.

the desk	der Schreibtisch	the book	das Buch
the school	die Schule	the chairs	die Stühle

Achtung bei der Aussprache: Wenn das nachfolgende Wort mit einem Vokallaut beginnt, wird *the* nicht /ðə/ ausgesprochen, sondern /ðiː/.

Der unbestimmte Artikel heißt im Englischen *a* und wird /ə/ ausgesprochen. Beginnt das nachfolgende Wort mit einem Vokallaut, verwendest du *an* /ən/.

a book   an exercise book   a uniform [ˈjuːnɪfɔːm]

8 DAS VERB HAVE GOT

the verb have got TB p. 151

Mit *have got* kann man ausdrücken, dass jemand etwas hat oder besitzt. Es gibt auch Kurzformen.

I / You / We / They have got a nice teacher.	→ I've got / You've got / We've got / They've got a nice teacher.
He / She / It has got a football.	→ He's / She's / It's got a football.

Wenn man sagen möchte, dass man etwas nicht hat, stellt man das Wort *not* zwischen *have* und *got* bzw. zwischen *has* und *got*. Die Kurzformen lauten *haven't* und *hasn't*.

I / You / We / They have not got two brothers.	→ I haven't got / You haven't got / We haven't got / They haven't got two brothers.
He / She / It has not got a football.	→ He hasn't / She hasn't / It hasn't got a football.

Wenn du eine Entscheidungsfrage mit *have got* bzw. *has got* stellen möchtest, stellst du *have* bzw. *has* an den Satzanfang. In der Kurzantwort wird dann *have* bzw. *has* wiederholt.

Have you got two brothers?	→ Yes, I have.	No, I haven't.
Has he / she / it got a football?	→ Yes, he / she / it has.	No, he / she / it hasn't.

Wenn du eine Frage mit Fragewort stellen willst, stellst du das Fragewort an den Anfang. Danach folgt dann *have* oder *has*.

What have you got? – I have got a bird.   Who has got a cat? – Tia has got a cat.

Das kenne ich schon (Seite 4)
1a: 1 green **2** purple **3** red **4** black **5** brown **6** white **7** yellow **8** pink **9** blue
1b: Individuelle Lösung
2: eight, eleven, six, three, twelve, one, seven, five, two, nine, four, ten.
3: Individuelle Lösung

Welcome

So many colours (Seite 5)
1: black, yellow, pink, green, orange, brown, blue, white, red, grey, purple

1, 2, 3, ... (Seite 5)
2a: 1 one **2** two **3** three **4** four **5** five **6** six **7** seven **8** eight **9** nine **10** ten **11** eleven
2b: 1 five, three **2** nine, eleven **3** ten, four

Farm animals (Seite 6)
3a: Individuelle Lösung
3b: 1 There are five white sheep. **2** The birds are blue. **3** There are two light brown cows. **4** There are three dark brown cows. **5** The cats are orange. **6** The horses are white and brown. **7** There are two birds. **8** There are two dogs. The dogs are grey. **9** There are nine rabbits. The rabbits are black and white.

The alphabet (Seite 7)
4: A red **B** green **C** yellow **D** blue **E** red **F** pink **G** orange **H** blue **I** black **J** green **K** red **L** yellow **M** orange **N** blue **O** white **P** black **Q** pink **R** blue **S** yellow **T** red **U** white **V** green **W** orange **X** black **Y** white **Z** yellow

New in Camden (Seite 7)
5a: 1 That's D–I–E–G–O **2** Where are you from? **3** I'm from London. **5** How old are you? **6** I'm eleven years old, too.

Unit 1

Part A: Me and my friends

Tia (Seite 8)
1a: (von oben nach unten) 5, 1, 2, 3, 7, 4, 6
1b: 1 brother, mum, dad **2** Camden, London **3** cat, guinea pig **4** orange juice **5** black, grey, white **6** music, dancing
2: [θ] thirteen, three, bath [ð] this, there, brother

Say it in English (Seite 9)
3: 1 What is your name? **2** Hi, my name is ... **3** Where are you from? **4** What's your favourite music?

Is she ...? / Are they ...? (Seite 9)
4: 1 Is **2** Are – Yes, I am. **3** Is – No, he isn't. **4** Is – Yes, she is. **5** Are – No, they aren't. **6** Are – Yes, they are. **7** Are – No, I'm not.

Countries (Seite 9)
5: 1 Germany, Deutschland **2** Great Britain, Großbritannien **3** Poland, Polen **4** Turkey, die Türkei **5** Italy, Italien **6** Denmark, Dänemark **7** Spain, Spanien

Who's she? What's that? (Seite 10)
6: 1 he = Tia's brother **2** it = house **3** They = Tia and her brother **4** it = guinea pig **5** she = Emma

Sebastian (Seite 10)
7: 1 You're **2** We're **3** They're **4** You are **5** She is **6** They are

Lena (Seite 10)
8: is not, is not, are not, is not, are not

Part B: My pets

What is it? (Seite 11)
1a: 1 dog **2** hamster **3** budgie **4** fish **5** cat **6** mouse

1b: 1 fruit **2** vegetables **3** water **4** mice
5 dog food
1c: Pets: fish, snake, mouse, cat, dog, guinea pig
Food: dog food, fruit, vegetables
Adjectives: cute, small, sweet, big, dangerous, friendly

Sneaky (Seite 11)
2: He is a snake. He is very big. He is a dangerous pet. He eats eggs and mice. He sleeps in a cage. He likes the cage.

My pet (Seite 12)
3: Beispiellösung: He is a cute and friendly dog. He eats meat and carrots. Ronald does tricks. He also swims and runs fast. He likes the park. He goes to the park with Megan.

What do the pets do everyday? (Seite 12)
4: 1 Sammy plays in the garden. **2** Fluffy watches birds. **3** Harry swims in water. **4** Benji eats carrots.

A homepage (Seite 13)
5: 1 is **2** is **3** likes **4** plays **5** eats **6** goes **7** sleeps
8 is **9** is **10** does tricks **11** runs **12** is **13** go
14 give **15** likes

Ask your classmates (Seite 13)
6a: Individuelle Lösung
6b: Individuelle Lösung

Part C: My home

An email from a friend (Seite 14)
1: **1** Sie sind blau. **2** Poster ihrer Lieblingsbasketballspieler, Regale **3** Es gibt drei **4** sehr groß und lila **5** einen Schreibtisch, Brettspiele, einen Korb für ihre Katze, einen Sessel **6** Ja, sie liebt es.

Where is it? (Seite 14)
2a: Individuelle Lösung
2b: Individuelle Lösung

His or her? (Seite 15)
3: our, her, our, Their, our, his, your

Tom's blue bed (Seite 15)
4: 1 Dolores' **2** Jim and Bob's **3** Laura's
4 Nicholas' **5** Toni's

A family quiz (Seite 15)
5: 1 c **2** f **3** b **4** d **5** a

Megan's family tree (Seite 16)
6a: 1 grandmother **2** Henry **3** mum **4** Ethan
5 sister **6** Adam
6b: Beispiellösung: Her brother is called Adam. Their parents are called Helen and Ethan. They are divorced. Ethan's parents are called Mary and John. Linda and Henry are Helen's parents. They are all Megan's grandparents.

Challenge (Seite 17)
Nilufar
1a: 1 She lives in Karachi. **2** She lives with her family. **3** They are 7 and 8 years old. **4** He likes to play with Nilufar and Arash. **5** Her favourite food is cherries and her favourite drink is tea.
1b: Age 11 **Place** Karachi **Hair colour** brown **Eye colour** brown **Brothers/Sisters** Arash and Meran **Pet** cat, Shahzadah **Likes** cricket **Favourite food** cherries **Favourite drink** tea

Checkout (Seite 18–19)
Speaking: Individuelle Lösung
Writing: Individuelle Lösung
Mediation: Beispiellösung: Zoes Bruder heißt Zack. Er ist 13 Jahre alt und er wohnt mit Zoe und ihren Eltern in London. Seine Lieblingsfarbe ist rot. Er hat eine rote Gitarre und er liebt Musik.

Reading: 1 right **2** wrong **3** wrong **4** right **5** not in the text **6** not in the text
Listening: 11, Regensburg, two sisters, no pets
Grammar: 1 my **2** His **3** our **4** my **5** my aunt's / her **6** Her **7** my aunt and uncle's/their **8** my uncle's / his
Vocabulary: 1 Germany **2** small **3** house **4** parents **5** yellow **6** bed **7** desk **8** On **9** desk **10** lamp **11** books **12** TV **13** computer

Unit 2

Part A: My school

Things and people at school (Seite 20)
1a: teacher, desk, pencil case, student, chair, ruler, scissors, whiteboard, book, pencil, pen
1b: Beispiellösung: The teacher is at the desk. The ruler is blue.
1c: 1 homework **2** exercise book **3** school bag **4** calendar **5** scissors **6** pencil case

More classroom phrases (Seite 20)
2: Can I open the window, please?
No John, it's too cold.
Can you spell it?
Can I have your ruler, please?
Yes, here you are.
Welcome to Haverstock school, Emma.

Ready for school (Seite 21)
3a: a folder, two exercise books, a ruler, two rubbers, five felt tips, three pens and three pencils.
3b: 1 thirteen **2** thirty **3** nineteen **4** twenty-eight **5** fifteen **6** twenty **7** twenty-one

Can they do it? (Seite 21)
4: 1 No, they can't. **2** No, you can't.
3 Yes, they can. **4** Yes, they can. **5** Yes, I can.

Have they got it? (Seite 22)
5: 1 has got, hasn't got **2** has got **3** have got **4** have got **5** hasn't got **6** haven't got

Look at him (Seite 22)
6: 1 her **2** them **3** him **4** me **5** it, me

A role play (Seite 22)
7: Individuelle Lösung

Part B: My timetable

A day at Haverstock School (Seite 23)
1 it feels like an early start to the weekend **2** at 11 o'clock and at 1 o'clock on Tuesday **3** Science **4** foreign language club **5** Tuesday **6** robotics club

1st, 2nd, 3rd, 4th ... (Seite 23)
2a: 1 third **2** eleventh **3** sixth **4** fifth **5** second **6** twenty-second **7** fourth **8** Individuelle Lösung
2b: You are in second place.

So many clocks (Seite 24)
3a: Individuelle Lösung
3b: 1 three o'clock **2** half past two **3** quarter past eight **4** two minutes past eleven

My Mondays (Seite 24)
4: Individuelle Lösung

My timetable (Seite 25)
5a: Individuelle Lösung
5b: Individuelle Lösung

They don't ... (Seite 25)
6: 1 don't want **2** doesn't forget **3** don't like **4** doesn't sleep **5** doesn't like

Part C: My way to school

How to get to school (Seite 26)
1: 1 train **2** car **3** by bus **4** on foot **5** Haverstock **6** hurry **7** classmates **8** bus stop **9** apologise

The breakfast table (Seite 26)
2: 1 spoon **2** fork **3** plate **4** tea **5** milk **6** juice **7** toast **8** jam
What do they like? (Seite 27)
3a: 1 Emma and Jack don't like tea. **2** Tia likes bananas. **3** Ben doesn't eat toast with jam. **4** Declan drinks orange juice. **5** The Hendersons don't eat cheese. **6** Ben loves chicken.
3b: 1 Does Emma play rugby? No, she plays basketball. **2** Where do the pupils meet? They meet at the bus stop. **3** Does Tia like drinking tea? No, she doesn't like drinking tea. **4** Do Ben and Declan like eating fruit? Yes, they like eating fruit.

Snow day? No way! (Seite 28)
5: 1 Ein Tag ohne Schule, weil es schneit.
2 Sie verbringt den ganzen Tag im Schnee. **3** mit einem Schneemobil **4** von November bis April
5 Man kommt zu Fuß oder mit einem Fahrrad dahin.

Sound Check (Seite 28)
[r] read, right, red, brother, write, hurry
[w] way, weekend, walk, window, wall, what

Challenge

School Expert (Seite 29)
1a: 1 Can I go to the toilet? **2** Which page are we on? **3** Can you open the window, please?
4 What's "Federmäppchen" in English?
5 I don't understand this exercise.
1b: 1 thirteen plus nineteen minus seven is twenty-five **2** eleven minus three plus fifteen is twenty-three **3** eighteen plus fourteen minus thirteen is nineteen
1c: 1 2.30 a.m. **2** 12.00 p.m. **3** 4.30 p.m. **4** 9.30 a.m. **5** 2.30 a.m.
Check out (Seite 30–31)
Speaking: Individuelle Lösung
Listening: 1 five **2** ICT **3** because she has PE early in the morning **4** French and ICT **5** RE
Reading: 1 right **2** wrong **3** wrong **4** right **5** wrong **6** not in the text **7** not in the text
Writing: Individuelle Lösung
Mediation: 1 ein Mathetest **2** einen schwarzen Stift, einen Bleistift und ein Lineal. Ein Radiergummi ist auch eine gute Idee.
3 man braucht kein Papier **4** einen blauen Stift
5 um 10 Uhr **6** pünktlich anzukommen
Grammar: 1 Mrs Newton doesn't teach Science. **2** We haven't got ten books. **3** Our school isn't in France. **4** I don't read a book every day.
5 He can't play football. **6** They don't like Maths.
Vocabulary: 1 fried egg **2** sausages **3** toast **4** butter **5** jam **6** tea **7** milk **8** orange juice

Unit 3

Part A: Festivals
Family, friends and festivals (Seite 32-33)
1a: 1 Tia's present is green. **2** Declan's present is blue. **3** Ben's present is yellow. **4** Emma's present is orange. **5** Jack's present is purple.
1b: 1 The Chopras' favourite festival is Diwali.
2 Nele's favourite festival is Pancake Day.
3 Tina's favourite festival is New Year. **4** The Woodins' favourite festival is Valentine's Day.
5 The children's favourite festival is Halloween.
1c: (von links nach rechts) 5, 3, /, 2, 0, 4

Christmas tongue twisters (Seite 33)
2: Individuelle Lösung

Kaan's presentation about Eid (Seite 33)
3: Thema: Eid
Präsentation von: Kaan
Religion: Islam
Dauer: Drei Tage
Wann: Jedes Jahr zu einem anderen Zeitpunkt
Anlass: um das Ende des Ramadan zu feiern
Wie man feiert: schicke Kleider tragen, in die

Moschee gehen, Großeltern besuchen
Glückwunsch: Eid Mubarak

What's going on? (Seite 34)
4a: Individuelle Lösung
4b: Beispiellösung: Sophie is wearing a pink dress. Emily is wearing a yellow sweatshirt, a green dress and blue shoes. Filip is wearing a red T-shirt and blue jeans. Alex is wearing a green sweatshirt and green trousers.

Part B: Shopping for a party (Seite 35)
Text message
1: 1 Sie fragt, ob ihre Oma und ihr Opa zur Party kommen. **2** Sie muss ausreichend Burger kaufen, weil er Burger gerne isst. **3** Sie hat ihre Handynummer nicht. **4** Sie soll ihren Vater nach der Nummer fragen. **5** Er ist nicht zu Hause. **6** Die Oma ruft Tias Mutter an.

Pounds and pence (Seite 35)
2: 1 £9.00 – nine pounds **2** £6.25 – six pounds twenty-five **3** £5.55 – five pounds fifty-five
4 £7.75 – seven pounds seventy-five
5 £9.01 – nine pounds one pence
6 £6.75 – six pounds seventy-five
7 £8.65 – eight pounds sixty-five

A Maths lesson (Seite 36)
3: Across: 3 forty **5** fifty **6** twenty **7** ninety **10** eighty **11** twelve **12** five **14** eleven
Down: 1 sixty **2** fifteen **4** thirty **8** eighteen **9** three **13** seventy

Sound check (Seite 36)
4: [æ] carrot, sandwich, fantastic, plan
[eɪ] paper, Friday, game, lemonade

The day after the party (Seite 37)
5a: 2 Is Rosie riding a horse? Yes, she is. **3** Are the parents working in the house? No, they are working in the garden. **4** Is Tom singing a song? Yes, he is. **5** Is Sophie using her computer? Yes, she is. **6** Is the family having breakfast? Yes, they are. **7** Is Zoe walking the dog? Yes, she is.
5b: Individuelle Lösung

Part C: Birthdays
At Tia's party (Seite 38)
1: 1 is getting buns **2** is taking the knives **3** is playing **4** are giving her **5** are eating **6** is opening **7** is chasing **8** is taking
2a: 1 third **2** first **3** fourth **4** sixth **5** second **6** sixth **7** fifth
2b: 1 the third balloon **2** the second pullover **3** the first present **4** the fourth party hat **5** the sixth coin **6** the fifth pair of sunglasses

Difficult words (Seite 39)
3: 1 one woman, two women **2** one sheep, two sheep **3** one child, two children **4** one knife, two knives **5** one foot, two feet **6** one baby, two babies **7** one fish, two fish

Tia's birthday muffins (Seite 40)
4a: Beispiellösung: Tia has got eggs, flour, sugar, a muffin tin and a spoon. Tia hasn't got butter, milk, dark chocolate or a big bowl.
4b: 1 g **2** c **3** f **4** e **5** a **6** d **7** b
4c: Individuelle Lösung

Challenge
There's something wrong (Seite 41)
1: 1 Are the girls dancing? No they aren't. They are playing cards. **2** Is the cat playing with a ball? No, it isn't. It is playing with a mouse. **3** Is the mum carrying a balloon? No, she isn't. She is carrying a cake. **4** Is the dad eating a hot dog? No, he isn't. He is eating a sandwich. **5** Are the boys playing football? No, they aren't. They are opening presents. **6** Is the dog wearing a red hat? No, it isn't. It is wearing a green hat. **7** Are the parents sleeping on the sofa? No, they aren't. They are standing in the dining room.

8 Is the dog playing cards? No, it isn't. It is drinking tea.

Checkout (Seite 42– 43)
Speaking: Individuelle Lösung
Mediation: 1 am 30. Oktober in der Schule **2** alle Schülerinnen und Schüler **3** zwei Pfund **4** Würste (auch vegetarisch) und Burger, sowie Pfannkuchen und Schokolade als Nachtisch
Reading: 1 right **2** wrong **3** right **4** right **5** not in the text
Writing: Individuelle Lösung
Listening: (von links nach rechts) 3, *Bild bleibt übrig*, 2, *Bild bleibt übrig*, 1, 4
Grammar: a) 1 No, she isn't. **2** Yes, she is. **3** No, she isn't. **4** No, they aren't.
b) 1 is reading **2** is drinking **3** is writing **4** am doing
Vocabulary: 1 ~~Monday~~ birthday **2** ~~bad~~ cool **3** ~~When~~ How **4** ~~pancakes~~ pounds

Unit 4

Part A: Hobbies
Blind football (Seite 44)
1: 1 Andy und seine Teammitglieder sind alle blind, bis auf den Torwart. **2** Der Fußball macht ein Geräusch, damit die Spieler wissen, wo der Fußball ist. **3** Eine Person hinter dem Tor sagt den Spielern, wo das Tor liegt. **4** Der Torwart sagt den Spielern, wo sie hinlaufen sollen. **5** Während des Spiels sind die Fans leise.

Word snake (Seite 44)
2: table tennis, riding, karate, travelling, computer games, climbing, inline skating

Bingo (Seite 45)
3: Individuelle Lösung
The friends and their hobbies (Seite 45)
4: 1 don't like playing **2** good at swimming **3** like playing **4** doesn't like dancing **5** like playing **6** is good at / likes / doesn't like playing hockey **7** hates playing

There are many hobbies (Seite 46)
5a: dancing, music, hockey, shopping, reading, swimming, football, chess, athletics, drama, yoga, computer
5b: Beispiellösung: I never play hockey. I sometimes go shopping. I always read. I usually listen to music. I often go swimming.

Carlos' free time (Seite 46)
6: 1 always **2** sometimes **3** often **4** often **5** never **6** usually **7** always

Part B: Doing sports
A terrible day on the hockey field (Seite 47)
1a: 1 goalkeeper **2** referee **3** miss **4** cheer **5** jersey
1b: 2 The game starts when the referee blows his whistle. **3** Jack and Ben are teammates. **4** Ben puts on his jersey in the changing room. **5** Jack can't stand playing as the goalkeeper. **6** After the foul, Jack gets a penalty.
1c: 1 their friends are watching **2** puts his hockey kit into his bag **3** Ben and Jack's coach is waiting **4** score a lot of goals **5** someone fouls Ben **6** Jack can take the penalty

During the match (Seite 48)
2: 1 e **2** b **3** d **4** a **5** c

Live ticker (Seite 48)
3: 1 sind aufgeregt **2** keine Tore **3** für Haverstock **4** um 15.47 Uhr **5** Er schießt einen Elfmeter. **6** niemand hat gewonnen

Free time activites (Seite 49)
4a: adverbials of place: im, in, zu Hause, draußen
adverbials of time: jeden Samstag, am Montag,

am Wochenende, Freitags, nach der Schule
4b: 1 Emma spends every Saturday in the dance studio. **2** On Monday she plays basketball at school. **3** Declan doesn't like stting at home at the weekend. **4** On Fridays, Tia helps at the Kentish Town Animal Shelter. **5** Ben plays board games at home at the weekend. **6** After school, Jack goes outside to play hockey.
4c: Individuelle Lösung
4d: Individuelle Lösung

Part C: Our weekend trip
At the farm (Seite 50)
1: 1 b **2** f **3** h **4** l **5** a **6** j **7** e **8** c **9** g **10** d

The trip to the farm (Seite 50)
2: 1 There are cows, pigs, ducks and chickens. **2** You can feed the chickens and look at the animals. **3** I like the piglets the most because they are cute. **4** There is a new baby cow.

Farm photos (Seite 51)
3a: Individuelle Lösung
3b: A 5 **B** 3 **C** 1 **D** 4 **E** 6 **F** 2
3c: 1 right **2** wrong **3** right **4** wrong **5** right **6** wrong **7** wrong
3d: Declan has got a photo of five pigs. Declan has got a photo of two horses on the farm. They are looking at photos of a newborn baby cow. Declan wants his parents to see the farm.

Gary's weekly routine (Seite 52)
4: simple present: usually, every Friday, always
present progressive: right now, now
1 am standing **2** sleeps **3** is **4** am going **5** am filling up **6** loves **7** jumps in **8** get

Bary is crazy (Seite 52)
5a: Beispiellösung: I can see Bary. He is standing in the water and he looks happy. There is Gary the farmer, too. He is angry. There are five people next to the field. They are laughing.
5b: Individuelle Lösung

Challenge
What do they do? (Seite 53)
1a: 1 She ~~never~~ is never late. **2** Declan sometimes goes ~~sometimes~~ swimming. **3** He usually practises ~~usually~~ the guitar.
1b: 1 Ben walks to training after lunch. **2** Emma and Tia go to the stadium at 4 p.m. **3** Declan's mum cooks a meal in the kitchen every day. **4** There is a hockey match near Haverstock School on Saturday.
1c: 1 Tia often helps at the shelter, but she is not helping today. **2** Emma is playing basketball now because she is always at training. **3** Jack sometimes shouts to Ben: 'Look, the ball is flying very high'. **4** Declan is never bored. He is enjoying the sun at the moment.

Check out (Seite 54– 55)
Speaking: Individuelle Lösung
Listening: tennis, field hockey, cricket
Reading: C, F, A, E, B
Writing: Individuelle Lösung
Mediation: regelmäßig: Ines = Hausaufgaben / Musik hören, ihr Bruder = in den Park gehen, Fußball spielen, ihre Schwester = zum Tennistraining gehen
gerade: Ines = schaut fern, ihr Bruder = einen Freund besuchen, Computerspiele spielen, ihre Schwester = sie schläft
Grammar: (von links nach rechts) 5, 4, 1, 2, 3
Vocabulary: 1 horse **2** chickens **3** cat **4** goat **5** cows **6** dog

Unit 5

Part A: This is Camden
More about Camden Market (Seite 56)
1: 4, 2, 1, 3
Two dream neighbourhoods (Seite 56)

2a: A, B, A, A, B, B, B, A, B, A, B
2b: Individuelle Lösung
2c: Individuelle Lösung

A lot to do in Camden (Seite 57)
3: 1 Camden Market **2** a new T-shirt **3** play football, eat ice cream later **4** go kayaking **5** Tia **6** Saturday.

On tour in Camden (Seite 57)
4: those, this, these, these, that, that, those, this

What is it? (Seite 58)
5: 1 building **2** market **3** cinema **4** street **5** house **6** gardens **7** zoo **8** temple
The letters in the purple boxes spell: museum

Can you or can't you? (Seite 58)
6: 1 can **2** can't, can / may **3** can **4** can **5** must

Part B: A horrible day in the city
Say it in English (Seite 59)
1a: 2 f **3** a **4** e **5** b **6** d
1b: 1 The accident happened on Camden High Street. **2** The e-scooter driver called for an ambulance. **3** The paramedics took Ben to the hospital. **4** They all went with Ben to the hospital. **5** The X-ray showed that Ben's leg is broken. **6** Ben was at the hospital only a few weeks ago because he hurt his shoulder at the hockey match.

Ben's email (Seite 59)
2a: 1 had **2** was **3** hit **4** fell over **5** cried **6** called **7** went **8** got **9** wanted **10** stopped
2b: Individuelle Lösung

The morning rap (Seite 60)
3: 2 – bed, 3 – teeth, 4 – head, 5 – bus, 6 – hands, 8 – feet

Body parts (Seite 60)
4a: Girl: (von oben nach unten) ear, nose, mouth, hand, finger, foot, toe, eye, face
Boy: (von oben nach unten) hair, tooth, back, stomach, bottom, knee, head, shoulder, arm, leg
4b: eyes, ears, feet, shoulders, toes, teeth, knees

Aliens (Seite 61)
5a: 2, 3, 1
5b: body parts: arms, nose, hair, feet, eyes, arms, feet, eye, teeth, legs
colours: yellow, green, red, blue, grey, brown, purple, black, orange, white, green
5c: Individuelle Lösung

Part C: A charity concert
A group chat (Seite 62)
1: 1 It still hurts. **2** The Barrow Boys **3** from the food trucks **4** not happy **5** the animal shelter **6** really full

Volunteering (Seite 62)
2: 1 um Tiere **2** Flyer verteilen **3** weil es hilft, Geld für die Organisation aufzutreiben. **4** Teenager sind willkommen. **5** Die RSPCA ist eine in England und Wales eingetragene Wohltätigkeitsorganisation.

Sound Check (Seite 63)
3a: Individuelle Lösung
3b: [ɪd] wanted, visited, texted, needed, completed [d] loved, enjoyed, planned, played, arrived [t] talked, walked, jumped, worked, looked

Last weekend (Seite 63)
4a: Individuelle Lösung
4b: 1 Emma and her brother were at a concert. **2** They did not watch TV. **3** They did not eat street food. **4** They went to the park. **5** They did not visit Camden Market. **6** They talked a lot.

Feelings (Seite 64)
5a: 1 happy **2** disappointed **3** excited **4** sad **5** ill
5b: Individuelle Lösung
Odd one out (Seite 64)
6: 1 animal shelter **2** food truck **3** bed **4** last year

Challenge
At Camden Market (Seite 65)
1: 1 can find **2** can't buy **3** can shop **4** can eat **5** can't go **6** can come

At the doctor (Seite 65)
2: Beispiellösung: 1 Patient 1 has got a broken arm. She should get a cast. **2** Patient 2 has got toothache. He shouldn't eat ice cream.
3 Patient 3 has got a stomach ache. She should stay in bed. **4** Patient 4 has got a headache. She shouldn't go to school. **5** Patient 5 is feeling dizzy. He should sit down.

Check out (Seite 66–67)
Speaking: Individuelle Lösung
Listening: 1 ~~cloudy~~ – sunny **2** ~~hot~~ – cold / cloudy **3** ~~warm and sunny~~ – rainy **4** ~~cold~~ – hot
Reading: 1 her aunt and uncle **2** at 8:30 a.m. **3** Tickets are free **4** history **5** they went to a Burger restaurant
Writing: Individuelle Lösung
Mediation: 1 SIe hat Fußball gespielt **2** Sie ist hingefallen. **3** ins Krankenhaus **4** so langweilig **5** ein bisschen besser / sie ist traurig wegen ihres Beins
Grammar: 1 Where did you go yesterday?
2 What did you eat? **3** Did you have dessert?
4 Who did you go with?
A 4 **B** 1 **C** 2 **D** 3
Vocabulary: Beispiellösung 1 <u>cricket</u> – school **2** <u>blue</u> – leg **3** <u>charity</u> – windy **4** <u>happy</u> – nervous

Unit 6

Part A: Holidays at home
Holiday activities at home (Seite 68)
1a: athletics, music, bike, yoga, volleyball, read, cinema, lake, park, cook, swim, museum
1b: Individuelle Lösung

Lisa and Holly's holidays (Seite 68–69)
2a: weather: warm, sunny, cold, rainy, nice
activities: stay up late, get up late, go swimming, ride my bike, meet my friends, go camping, visit sights, go hiking, play volleyball
2b: weather: warm, cold, rainy **activities:** read, listen to music, meet friends, play outside, go swimming, stay in bed all day
2c: warm and sunny: go hiking, go swimming, meet friends, ride bikes, play volleyball, play outside **cold and rainy:** stay in bed, visit museums, visit castles **all weather:** read, listen to music

At the skate park (Seite 69)
3: 1 Nein, man darf nur Skateboard, Inline-skates oder Scooter fahren **2** Ja, weil du unter 16 Jahre alt bist. **3** Glasbehälter sind verboten **4** von der Abenddämmerung bis zum Morgengrauen

Orla's dream holiday (Seite 70)
4: 1 Please don't give me jobs at home. **2** Please go swimming with me. **3** Please make dinner.
4 Please play board games with me. **5** Please don't wake me up.

Part B: Holidays in Britain
Where are you going this summer? (Seite 71)
1: 1 his grandma **2** eat lots of ice cream **3** to museums **4** It is cheap. **5** She can sleep in her own bed. **6** eating and hiking

Cornish Adventure Camp (Seite 71)
2: 1 in Newquay **2** Bodyboarding und Surfen
3 Man kann das Aquarium besuchen.
4 28. Juli – 4. August und 14. August – 21. August
5 Es kostet £768.

A postcard from Wales (Seite 72)
3: 1 and **2** but **3** because **4** because **5** or **6** and **7** and

Holiday plans (Seite 72-73)
4a: 1 are going **2** are staying **3** am visiting **4** are getting **5** are driving **6** is hiking **7** are having **8** walking **9** are going
4b: 1 sunglasses **2** phone **3** trousers **4** towel **5** pullover **6** diary
4c: Individuelle Lösung

On the way (Seite 73)
5: 2 Lisa's family drive to Scotland by car. **3** Mr Smith goes to work by train. **4** Tia flies to Cyprus by plane **5** Declan goes to Brighton by bus.

Part C: Holiday abroad
What's Happening? (Seite 74)
1: (von links nach rechts) 2 – The friends are practising bodyboarding on the beach. 4 – Jack is walking away from the water. 7 – The friends see Jack. 3 – The friends are running into the water with their bodyboards. 6 – The friends are looking for Jack. 8 – Jack is sitting on the beach and is drawing a picture. 5 – The friends see that Jack is not there. 1 – The four friends are walking on the beach.

On the beach (Seite 75)
2a: Individuelle Lösung
2b: Individuelle Lösung

Getting information abroad (Seite 75)
3: 1 When and where is breakfast? **2** How do I get to the beach? **3** Where is the nearest bus stop? **4** How much do a postcard and a stamp to Germany cost?

Weather poems (Seite 76)
4: Individuellle Lösung

Packing my suitcase (Seite 76)
5: 1 hiking sticks, hiking boots, sunglasses, surfboard, cap, T-shirt, shorts, sunscreen, swimsuit, goggles **2** hiking sticks, raincoat, hiking boots, sunglasses, shorts, T-shirt, cap, sunscreen, coat, pullover **3** scarf, gloves, winter hat, pullover, coat, snowboard, sunscreen, raincoat

Challenge
Visiting Germany (Seite 77)
1a: the Kaiserburg, Lebkuchen, the Zoo in Nuremberg
1b: 1 – June arrived in Nuremburg on Saturday.
2 – They stayed inside and played board games.
3 – June was bored and went to the kitchen.
4 – On Sunday morning they visited a castle.
5 – After the walk they bought a speciality from Nuremburg. 6 – Then they went to the zoo.
1c: Individuelle Lösung

Check out (Seite 78–79)
Speaking: Individuelle Lösung
Listening: (von links nach rechts) 2, 3, 1, 4, 5
Mediation: 1 Sie geht mit ihrer Schwester shoppen. **2** Sie fahren ans Meer. **3** Um 14 Uhr
Writing: Individuelle Lösung
Reading: a) The text is about a holiday destination in England.
b) 1 in the north-west of England **2** tigers and elephants **3** fish and chips **4** a museum **5** a big amusement park
Grammar: 1 He is cleaning the room. **2** They are baking a cake. **3** They are going abroad. **4** She is walking the dog.
Vocabulary: 1 travelling by plane **2** uncle **3** hot **4** shorts **5** ice cream

9 DIE VERLAUFSFORM DER GEGENWART: AUSSAGEN

present progressive: statements TB p. 152

Wenn du ausdrücken möchtest, dass jemand etwas jetzt gerade tut oder dass etwas in diesem Moment stattfindet, kannst du das mit dem *present progressive* tun. Du bildest es mit einer Form von *be* sowie der Grundform des Verbs *+ing*. Signalwörter für die Verwendung des *present progressive* sind zum Beispiel *at the moment, (right) now, today und this week.*

I am wrapping presents at the moment.
You are talking to me.

Declan's mum is decorating the living room.
Aunt Valerie and Uncle Eric are having a cup of tea.

Für die Verneinung fügst du *not* hinter der Form von *be* ein. Hier wird dann häufig die Kurzform verwendet.

I am not making pizza.	→ I'm not making pizza.
She is not buying crisps.	→ She isn't buying crisps.
They are not dancing.	→ They aren't dancing.

10 DIE VERLAUFSFORM DER GEGENWART: FRAGEN

present progressive: questions TB p. 153

Mit dem *present progressive* kannst du fragen, was jemand gerade tut. Bei Entscheidungsfragen stellst du eine Form von *be* an den Satzanfang. Man antwortet darauf meist mit einer Kurzantwort.

Am I dreaming?	Yes, you are.	No, you aren't.
Are you doing your homework?	Yes, I am.	No, I'm not.
Is he/she/it playing?	Yes, he/she/it is.	No, he/she/it isn't.
Are they dancing?	Yes, they are.	No, they aren't.

Bei Fragen mit Fragewort steht das Fragewort am Satzanfang.

What are you doing?
Where are you going?

11 DIE PLURALFORMEN DER NOMEN

the plural forms of nouns TB p. 154

Die meisten englischen Nomen haben im Plural die Endung -s. Achte auf die unterschiedliche Aussprache.

a fork one bun	two forks /-s/ four buns /-z/	Nach stimmlosen Konsonanten klingt das *-s* wie ein Zischen, nach stimmhaften Konsonanten wie ein Summen.
a story my hobby	two stories /-ɪz/ my hobbies /-ɪz/	Steht ein Konsonant vor einem *-y*, so wird das *-y* im Plural zu *-ies*.
a bus a sandwich	two buses /-ɪz/ two sandwiches /-ɪz/	Nomen, die auf *-s, -ss, -sh, -ch* oder *-x* enden, erhalten im Plural ein *-es*.
one foot a child	two feet lots of children	Unregelmäßige Pluralformen lernst du am besten zusammen mit der Singularform.

12 DAS GERUNDIUM

the gerund TB p. 155

Wird ein Verb wie ein Nomen verwendet, nennt man das Gerundium. Im Englischen benutzt du dafür die *ing*-Form des Verbs.

Das Gerundium kann im Englischen nach bestimmten Ausdrücken wie *like, love, hate, to be good/bad at* und *can't stand* stehen:

Emma loves reading books.
Tia is good at riding horses.
Declan can't stand sitting at home.

Das Gerundium kann auch das Subjekt eines Satzes sein. Du fragst danach mit *wer* oder *was*?

Swimming is fun.
My favourite hobby is playing the drums.

13 HÄUFIGKEITSADVERBIEN

adverbs of frequency TB p. 156

Wörter wie *always, usually, often, sometimes* und *never* sind Häufigkeitsadverbien. Mit ihnen kannst du ausdrücken, wie häufig etwas geschieht.

I always practise running on Fridays.
Ben's dad sometimes cleans the bathroom.

My parents often do the cooking.
You never help!

Bei Sätzen mit *be* stehen die Formen von *be* vor dem Adverb.

I am always hungry.
He is often at home on Sunday mornings.

We are usually in the park on Fridays.
It is never boring at the swimming pool.

Dustys Hinweis

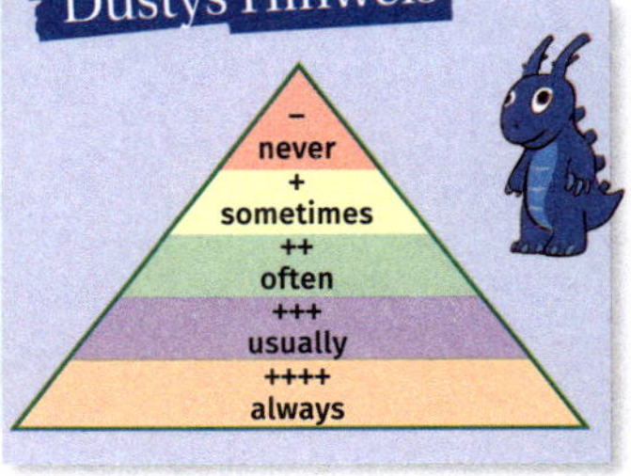

14 DIE WORTSTELLUNG IM SATZ

word order in statements TB p. 157

Aussagesätze werden nach einem bestimmten Muster gebildet: Subjekt - Verb - Objekt (S - V - O). Danach können noch weitere Ergänzungen stehen.

Subjekt	Verb	Objekt	Ergänzung
Jack	eats	his cereal.	
He	eats	it	in the kitchen in the morning.

Mehrere Sätze können mit *linking words* verbunden werden. Die Konjunktionen *and*, *or* und *but* verbinden zwei Hauptsätze und die Konjunktion *because* verbindet einen Haupt- und einen Nebensatz:

You can go out to sea by boat *[1. Hauptsatz]* **or** you can try hang-gliding. *[2. Hauptsatz]*
Seaside towns are very popular *[Hauptsatz]* **because** the beaches are beautiful. *[Nebensatz]*

15 MODALVERBEN

modal verbs TB p. 158

Mit Modalverben kannst du ausdrücken, was jemand tun kann, darf oder muss. Auf Modalverben folgt immer ein anderes Verb im Infinitiv.

I can speak German.
I can't find my English folder.
Can you help me, please? — Yes, I can. — No, I can't.
When can we go to the park? — You can go there in the afternoon.
May I use your phone?
You may use a dictionary in the test.
You must leave your shoes outside.

Dustys Hinweis
Achtung: ***must not / mustn't*** bedeutet „nicht dürfen", auch wenn es wie „nicht müssen" klingt!

16 DIE EINFACHE VERGANGENHEIT: AUSSAGEN

the simple past: statements TB p. 159

Wenn du über etwas sprechen willst, das in der Vergangenheit liegt und abgeschlossen ist, verwendest du die einfache Vergangenheit *(simple past)*. Bei regelmäßigen Verben bildest du es, indem du die Endung *-ed* an die Grundform anhängst. Die Formen der unregelmäßigen Verben musst du lernen.

My friends listened to good music at the concert.
They went to the concert yesterday.

I was at the hospital.
My friends were at the church.

Die Verneinung im *simple past* bildest du bei allen Personen mit *didn't* (= *did not*). Danach kommt dann das Verb in der Grundform. Bei *was* und *were* hängst du *not* oder die Kurzform *n't* an, wenn du einen verneinten Satz bilden willst.

I didn't eat food from the food truck.
Declan didn't see The Protractors yesterday.

I wasn't at the concert last week.
The Protractors weren't at the concert.

17 DIE EINFACHE VERGANGENHEIT: FRAGEN

the simple past: questions TB p. 160

Bei Entscheidungsfragen im *simple past* stellst du *did* an den Satzanfang. *Did* ist bei allen Personen gleich. Danach folgt das Verb in der Grundform. In der Kurzantwort wird *did* wieder aufgegriffen.

Entscheidungsfrage	Kurzantwort	Kurzantwort
Did you all go to the concert?	Yes, we did.	No, we didn't.
Did Declan eat too much?	Yes, he did.	No, he didn't.

Bei Fragen mit *was* und *were* brauchst du kein *did*. Hier steht *was* oder *were* am Satzanfang. In der Kurzantwort wird *was* oder *were* wieder aufgegriffen: Was the hospital food good? Yes, it was./No, it wasn't.

Bei Fragen mit Fragewort steht das Fragewort am Satzanfang: **What** did you eat yesterday? **Where** did you go?

Wenn *who* nach dem Subjekt fragt, brauchst du kein zusätzliches *did*: **Who** went to the concert?

Auch bei Fragen mit *was* und *were* brauchst du kein *did*: **How** was the concert? **What** were the bands like?

18 DIE BEFEHLSFORM

the imperative TB p. 161

So kannst du jemanden um etwas bitten oder auffordern, etwas zu tun (Befehlsform):

Help me!
Come to the pool, please.
Hurry up, please.
Meet me at the lockers, please.

Wenn jemand etwas *nicht* tun soll, kannst du das so sagen (verneinte Befehlsform):

Don't run!
Don't forget your swimsuit.
Don't be too loud.
Don't play use lilos in the pool, please.

Bingo

3 wordbank: free time TB p. 188

Write down eight different hobbies in the boxes. Your classmates present their favourite hobby. When you hear a hobby that is in one of your boxes, tick it off. The first person to tick three hobbies in a row (up, down, across or diagonally) is the winner.

football		

The friends and their hobbies

4 grammar in short: 12 gerund

Complete the sentences about the friends. What do they like (😃), not like (☹️), or hate (😬)? What are they good at (✓)?

hobbies	Tia	Jack	Ben	Declan	Emma
riding a horse	✓	☹️	☹️	☹️	☹️
playing hockey	😬	✓	😃	☹️	☹️
playing e-football	☹️	😬	✓	😬	😬
playing board games	😃	☹️	😃	😬	😃
playing an instrument	😃	☹️	☹️	😃	✓
swimming	☹️	😃	😃	✓	☹️
dancing	😃	😬	☹️	☹️	😃
playing basketball	☹️	😃	😃	😃	✓

0 Tia ______ *is good at riding* ______ a horse.

1 Jack and Ben ______________________ an instrument.

2 Declan is ______________________ .

3 Emma and Tia ______________________ board games.

4 Declan ______________________ .

5 The boys ______________________ basketball.

6 Only one boy ______________________ hockey.

7 Jack ______________________ e-football.

There are many hobbies

5a

Find twelve of the new hobby words from pages 76–81 in your textbook.

d	a	s	h	o	c	k	e	y	g	i	l	s	w	d	r	a	h	p	s	f
a	s	h	o	p	p	i	n	g	m	p	v	t	q	u	o	y	o	g	a	g
n	a	m	l	e	y	z	g	t	w	n	c	i	n	e	m	a	s	u	i	y
c	b	u	r	e	a	d	z	d	g	w	t	b	l	m	x	c	w	t	l	d
i	p	s	p	s	w	i	m	m	i	n	g	i	s	a	m	n	f	k	l	v
n	t	i	e	s	f	o	o	t	b	a	l	l	c	o	m	p	u	t	e	r
g	d	c	k	u	c	h	e	s	s	a	t	h	l	e	t	i	c	s	y	p

5b grammar in short: 13 adverbs of frequency

Make sentences with words from 5a and from the box.

I often go to the cinema.

often · never · sometimes · usually · always

Carlos' free time

6 grammar in short: 13 adverbs of frequency

Read what Carlos says about his free time. Fill in the right *adverbs of frequency* (textbook page 81).

New Message

To: myfriends@camdenroad.com

Subject: Carlos from Mexico says hi

Hi, I'm Carlos. I'm 11 years old and I live in Mexico City. I speak Spanish, of course, but my favourite subject at school is English. I ________ (++++) read comics and they are ________ (+) in English. My aunt and uncle live in the USA and they ________ (++) send me comics and sweets. I also love playing football. My friends and I ________ (++) play in the street or in the park. I ________ (–) play on my own – it's more fun with friends! I'm good at dancing, too. I ________ (+++) practise every Tuesday after school. And I ________ (++++) dance at family parties!

A terrible day on the hockey field

1a

What can you see? Write down the hockey words. The text on textbook page 82 can help you.

1

____

2

____

3

____

4

____

5
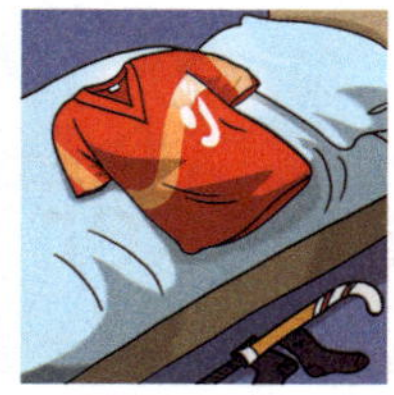
____

1b

Match the parts of the sentences. The text on textbook page 82 can help you.

1 Emma	playing as the	the changing room.
2 The game	wants tickets for	blows his whistle.
3 Jack and Ben	are	the hockey game.
4 Ben puts on	starts when the referee	goalkeeper.
5 Jack can't stand	his jersey in	penalty.
6 After the foul, Jack	gets a	teammates.

1c skill: reading TB p. 166

Read the text on page 82 in your textbook again. Then tick (✓) the right sentence ending.

1 Jack and Ben are excited because

- ☐ they don't want to lose.
- ☐ the boys are at their neighbouring school.
- ☐ their friends are watching.

2 After he eats his breakfast, Jack

- ☐ cleans the kitchen.
- ☐ puts his hockey things into his bag.
- ☐ rides his bicycle to Ben.

3 When they arrive at the hockey field

- ☐ Ben and Jack's coach is waiting.
- ☐ the players are on the field.
- ☐ the friends are nervous.

4 Jack and Ben want to

- ☐ make a loud noise.
- ☐ talk to the other team.
- ☐ score a lot of goals.

5 The referee blows the whistle because

- ☐ someone fouls Ben.
- ☐ Emma shouts too loud.
- ☐ Ben is crying.

6 The coach decides that

- ☐ Ben can take the penalty.
- ☐ the goalkeeper looks nervous.
- ☐ Jack can take the penalty.

During the match

2 audio 2/14, skill: listening TB p. 165

Listen to the dialogues. Who thinks what? Match the dialogues and the names.

1 Emma ______ 2 Ben ______ 3 Jack ______ 4 coach ______ 5 goalkeeper ______

Live ticker

3 skill: mediation TB p. 168

Lies den Liveticker zum Spiel. Beantworte die Fragen stichpunktartig auf Deutsch. Ein Wort genügt nicht.

2.30 p.m.	Welcome to our live coverage of today's hockey match: Haverstock United vs. Whitehall Wolves. The teams are already arriving and the fans are finding their seats. Everybody is very excited!
2.55 p.m.	The teams are coming out onto the field. The referee is following with the ball. The fans are cheering!
3 p.m.	The referee blows his whistle: Face off!
3.15 p.m.	The end of the first quarter and no goals: a boring match so far!
3.25 p.m.	8 minutes into the second quarter and Jack Henderson is running towards the goal. He almost scores for Haverstock. But no, he misses!
3.32 p.m.	Half time and the score is still 0–0. See you in 15 minutes!
3.47 p.m.	Welcome back to the second half of Haverstock vs. Whitehall, where the score is 0–0.
4.18 p.m.	The final minute of the match and the referee blows his whistle. Foul! A Haverstock player is lying on the ground. He needs a stretcher. That means a penalty for Haverstock!
4.20 p.m.	Jack Henderson takes the penalty for Haverstock. He misses!
4.21 p.m.	The whistle blows and the match is over. The score is 0–0. Both teams are leaving the field sad and disappointed.

1 Wie fühlen sich die Spieler und Fans vor dem Spiel?

______

2 Warum ist das Spiel am Ende des ersten Viertels langweilig?

______

3 Für welche Mannschaft spielt Jack Henderson?

______

4 Wann fängt die zweite Hälfte des Spiels an?

______

5 Was macht Jack nach dem Foul?

______

6 Warum verlassen beide Mannschaften das Feld traurig?

______

Free time activities

4a
grammar in short: 14 word order in statements

Read the sentences in 4b. Underline each *adverbial of place* blue and each *adverbial of time* green.

4b

Write the sentences in English. Be careful: In English the word order is sometimes different.

1 Emma verbringt jeden Samstag im Tanzstudio.

2 Sie spielt am Montag Basketball in der Schule.

3 Declan mag es nicht, am Wochenende zu Hause zu sitzen.

4 Freitags hilft Tia im Kentish Town Animal Shelter.

5 Ben spielt am Wochenende Brettspiele zu Hause.

6 Nach der Schule geht Jack nach draußen zum Hockey spielen.

4c

What do you do in your free time? Where and when do you do it? Complete the table.

Who?	What?	Where?	When?
	play board games	*at home*	*after school*
I			

4d

Get together with a partner. Talk about what you do in your free time.

You can ask:

What do you do after school?

Where do you meet your friends?

You can answer:

After school I play football.

I meet them in the park at the weekend.

At the farm

1 skill: reading TB p. 166

Read the text on page 86 in your textbook again. Match the sentence halves.

1 The four friends ☐
2 Jack and his friends enjoy ☐
3 A duckling ☐
4 Emma is looking for ☐
5 Tia says that ☐
6 There's something wrong ☐
7 The children must be quiet ☐
8 Molly is scared ☐
9 Molly's baby ☐
10 Emma wants to take a photo ☐

A the piglets are cute.
B go to Kentish Town City Farm.
C because it's her first baby.
D of the baby cow and the friends.
E because Molly is scared.
F feeding the chickens.
G stands up for the first time.
H follows Jack.
I the duckling's family.
J with Molly.

The trip to the farm

2 skill: writing TB p. 167

Tia's friends want to know more about the farm. Scan the text on textbook page 86 and write down Tia's answers.

Dusty explains
If you scan a text, you look for important information, for example special facts. You go through the text quickly. You don't read every word.

1 What animals are there on the farm?

____

____

2 What can you do on the farm?

____

____

3 Tia, what animals do you like most? Why?

____

____

4 You look very excited. Can you tell me anything special about the day?

____

____

Farm photos

3a

Look at Declan's photos in 3b. Work with a partner. Choose a photo and talk about it. Your partner has to guess which one it is. Take turns.

You can say:

There is … / There are …

I can see …

3b audio 2/16, skill: listening TB p. 165

Listen to Declan. In what order does he talk about the photos?

A

B

C

D

E

F

A ______

B ______

C ______

D ______

E ______

F ______

3c audio 2/16

Listen again. Are the statements right or wrong? Tick (✓) the right box.

	right	wrong
1 Declan's family are looking at photos of Kentish Town City Farm.	☐	☐
2 Declan has got a photo of three pigs.	☐	☐
3 He has got a photo of a duckling.	☐	☐
4 Declan has got a photo of three horses on the farm.	☐	☐
5 He thinks that goats are boring.	☐	☐
6 They are looking at photos of a newborn baby goat.	☐	☐
7 Declan doesn't want his parents to see the farm.	☐	☐

3d

Listen again and correct the wrong sentences from 3c.

______

______

______

______

Gary's weekly routine

4 grammar in short: 4 simple present + 9 present progressive

Highlight the signal words for *simple present* orange and the signal words for *present progressive* purple. Then fill in the right verb forms.

Right now, I ______________ (stand) in front of Bary, the bull. He usually ______________ (sleep) for a long time, but every Friday ______________ (be) his bath day. Now I ______________ (go) into his field and I ______________ (fill up) the pond with water. He ______________ (love) water. When the water is ready, he always ______________ (jump in). Then I usually ______________ (get) wet.

Bary is crazy

5a grammar in short: 9 present progressive, skill: describing pictures TB p. 172

What can you see in the picture? Write at least two sentences in the *present progressive*.

I can see Bary. He is standing in the water and he looks happy. There is …

5b

Read the text and draw a picture.

You can see three bulls.
Two of them are eating green grass and one wants to jump over the high fence.
In the sky, the sun is shining.
On the right, there is a tree.
In the tree, a yellow bird is singing.

What do they do?

1a grammar in short: 13 adverbs of frequency

Cross out the words in the wrong positions. Then write down the right sentences.

0 Tia often helps ~~often~~ at the animal shelter. *Tia often helps at the animal shelter.*

1 She never is never late. ______

2 Declan sometimes goes sometimes swimming. ______

3 He usually practises usually the guitar. ______

1b grammar in short: 14 word order in statements

Unscramble the sentences. Be careful! There are some *adverbs of time and place*.

1 after lunch / Ben walks / to training

______

2 the stadium / Emma and Tia / go to / at 4 p.m.

______

3 cooks / a meal / Declan's mum / in the kitchen / every day

______

4 on Saturday / there is / a hockey match / near Haverstock School

______

1c grammar in short: 4 simple present + 9 present progressive + 14 word order in statements

Unscramble the parts of the sentences in brackets. Then write the sentences. Use the *simple present* or the *present progressive*. The signal words can help you.

1 (Tia / help / at the shelter / often), but (she / not / help) today.

______

2 (Emma / play / basketball / now) because (she / be / at training / always).

______

3 (Jack / shout / to Ben / sometimes): "(Look, / the ball / fly / very high!)"

______

4 (Declan / be / bored / never). (He / enjoy / the sun / at the moment).

______

Check out

Speaking solutions p.83

Talk to a partner. Ask each other questions about your free time. You can use the pictures for ideas. Take turns.

You can ask:

What do you do in your free time?
Where do you do that?
When do you do it?
Who do you do it with?

You can answer:

I often play the guitar.
I usually do it in my room.
...

Ich kann: über meine Hobbys sprechen. ○
mich über meine Freizeit unterhalten. ○

Listening audio 2/21, solutions p.83

Listen to Michael. Tick (✓) the three sports he likes doing.

- ☐ tennis
- ☐ field hockey
- ☐ rugby
- ☐ football
- ☐ darts
- ☐ cricket

Ich kann: einen Hörtext zum Thema "Sport" verstehen. ○

Reading solutions p.83

Where do these sentences fit in the text? Find the best place and write the letters A, B, C, D, E or F in the box. Be careful, there are more letters than you need.

Let me tell you about my friends. Annabel loves cooking. She cooks every weekend. ☐ Will enjoys playing football. ☐ Chrissie is a very quiet person. She likes sitting in her bedroom and reading. ☐ My brother is a very loud person. He loves music. ☐ Oh, and what about me? Well, I am a creative person. ☐ What is your hobby?

- **A** She is reading a book about a dragon at the moment.
- **B** I like drawing pictures of trees.
- **C** She loves cooking spaghetti Bolognese.
- **D** She plays the piano after school.
- **E** He plays the guitar.
- **F** He loves PE at school.

Ich kann: verstehen, wann, wo und wie oft jemand etwas tut. ○

Writing solutions p.83

Write about your free time. Use the *adverbs of frequency* in the box. Write 30-50 words.

always · usually · often · sometimes · never

You can write:

I never play the piano, but I sometimes play the guitar.
I often go ...

Ich kann: über meine Hobbys schreiben. ○ sagen, wie oft ich etwas tue. ○

Mediation solutions p. 83

Lies, was Ines sagt. Vervollständige die Tabelle stichpunktartig auf Deutsch. Ein Wort genügt nicht.

After school, I usually do my homework. I like listening to music, too. I don't have any homework today, so right now I am watching TV in the living room. My brother often goes to the park with his friends and plays football. But it is raining today so he is visiting his best friend and they are playing video games. My sister often goes to tennis practice after school. But today she is ill so she is sleeping.

Wer?	Was macht er / sie regelmäßig?	Was macht er / sie gerade?
Ines		
ihr Bruder		
ihre Schwester		

Ich kann: die Zeitformen für regelmäßig oder gerade stattfindende Dinge verstehen. ◯

USE OF ENGLISH

Grammar solutions p. 83

Read the text. Rank Mia's activities from 1 (most often) to 5 (never).

Mia likes doing lots of activities. Her favourite hobby is playing the guitar. She plays the guitar every day after school. Her brother likes playing football, but she hates it so she never plays it. She likes listening to music. She sometimes listens to music in the morning on the way to school. She also enjoys cooking, but she often doesn't have time to cook. She cooks once a month. She also loves watching films. She usually watches a film twice a week.

☐  ☐  ☐ 

☐  ☐ 

Vocabulary solutions p. 83

Write down the missing words.

John is a farmer. He has lots of animals. His favourite animal is his ______________ , Rosie. He cleans her stable every day. He also has lots of ______________ . They often escape, so he has to run after them! He has a black ______________ . Her name is Jess. He feeds Jess in the morning. Billy is a ______________ . He lives on the farm, too. And let's not forget about the ________ . They enjoy being outside on the field. In the evening, he feeds his ______________ , Spot. Then they play together.

Ich kann: sagen, wie oft jemand etwas tut. ◯ Tiere auf Englisch benennen. ◯

More about Camden Market

1 skill: reading TB p. 166

Match the questions about Camden Market and the right information below.

1 On what days is Camden Market open?
2 How do I get to Camden Market?
3 What are the opening times?
4 What can I do at Camden Market?

☐ Camden Market has more than 1,000 places to shop, eat, drink and dance. Find clothing and gift ideas, or simply get something to eat at one of many cafes, bars and street food stalls.

☐ To get to Camden Market on the underground, you can take the Northern Line to Camden Town or Chalk Farm station. To get to Camden Market by bus, you can take bus number 24, 124, 274 or 393.

☐ Camden Market is open seven days a week, including all bank holidays. The market is also open some evenings.

☐ Camden Market is open from 10 a.m. to 6 p.m.

Two dream neighbourhoods

2a skill: reading TB p. 166

These texts about two dream neighbourhoods are mixed up. Sort them out. Write A or B next to the sentences.

☐ In my dream neighbourhood, everything is green!
☐ My dream neighbourhood is on another planet.
☐ There are lots of trees and parks.
☐ We don't have cars. We have bikes and horses.
☐ There aren't any cars. People use flying skateboards.
☐ The houses are tall and grey and look like spaceships.
☐ There are robots.
☐ People live in trees.
☐ The sky is black and full of stars.
☐ I love my green neighbourhood!
☐ There are computers everywhere. I love it!

A

B

2b

Which dream neighbourhood from 2a do you like best? Why?

2c skill: writing TB p. 167

Describe your own dream neighbourhood.

A lot to do in Camden

3 audio 2/25, skill: listening TB p. 165

Listen to Ben and Tia. Tick (✓) the right answers.

1 Where do the two friends want to go first?

- [ ] Regent's Canal
- [ ] Regent's Park
- [ ] Camden Market

2 What does Tia want to buy?

- [ ] a new book
- [ ] a new skateboard
- [ ] a new T-shirt

3 What do the friends want to do later?

- [ ] play football
- [ ] eat ice cream
- [ ] watch TV

4 What can you do at Pirate Castle?

- [ ] go swimming
- [ ] go shopping
- [ ] go kayaking

5 Who wants to go to Pirate Castle?

- [ ] Ben
- [ ] Tia
- [ ] Ben and Tia

6 When do Ben and Tia want to meet?

- [ ] Friday
- [ ] Saturday
- [ ] Sunday

On tour in Camden

4

Emma and Tia are on a tour in Camden with Emma's brother. Circle the right words.

Look at **this / these / those** boats over there on Regent's Canal. We could do a tour. And **this / that / these** here is Camden Market. **This / These / Those** stalls sell food and from **this / these / those** stalls here you can get cool clothes. Let's eat something. Maybe we can ask **those / that / these** guy about his pizza. It looks really yummy! And then we can go to the zoo. It's **this / that / these** building over there. Can you see the animals on the sign? **This / Those / These** are giraffes. But first of all, I want to have a look in **that / these / this** shop here.

What is it?

5 wordbank: places TB p. 189

Complete the crossword. What place do the letters in the purple boxes spell?

1 something with walls and a roof

2 a place where you can buy and sell things

3 a place where you can go to watch a film

4 a road in a town or city that has houses or other buildings

5 a place where families or people live

6 a park or large area where plants and flowers grow

7 a place where you can see lots of wild animals

8 a building which people in some religions visit

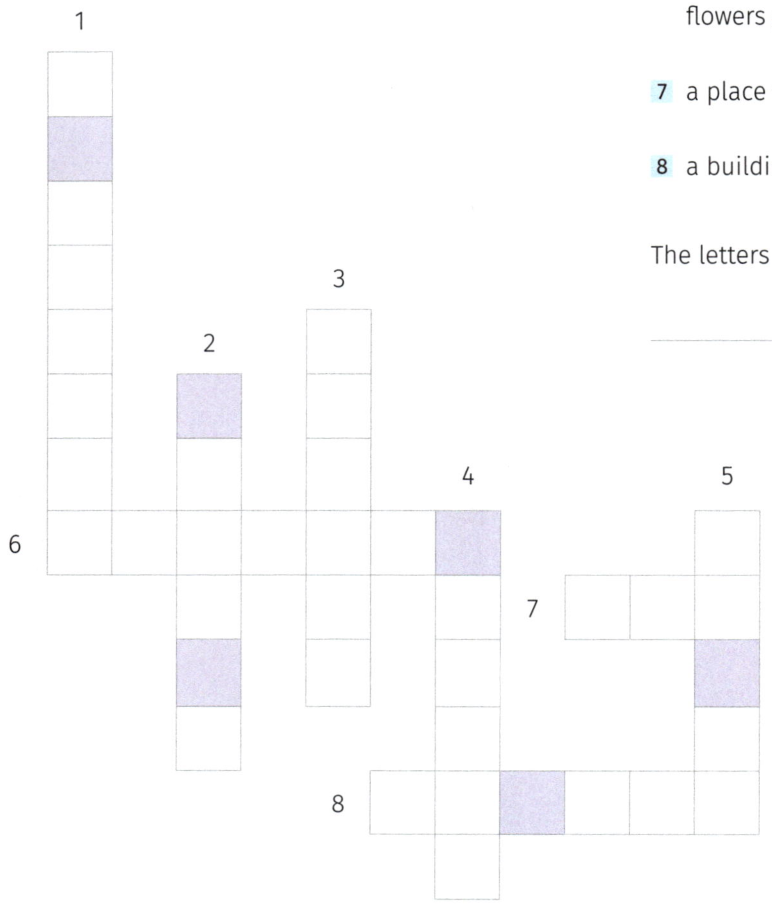

The letters in the purple boxes spell

______________________________ .

Can you or can't you?

6 grammar in short: 15 modal verbs

Complete the sentences with *can, can't, may* or *must*.

1 You ______________ buy second-hand clothes at Camden Market.

2 You ______________ play with the animals at London Zoo, but you ______________ feed them.

3 You ______________ use the bus, train or underground to travel around London.

4 Everyone ______________ visit the British Museum for free!

5 You ______________ be careful when you use the underground.

Say it in English

1a

Match the German and English questions.

1 Where did the accident happen?
2 Who called for an ambulance?
3 Where did the paramedics take Ben?
4 Who went with Ben to the hospital?
5 What did the X-ray show?
6 Why was Ben at the hospital only a few weeks ago?

A Wohin haben die Rettungssanitäter Ben gebracht?
B Was war auf dem Röntgenbild?
C Wo ist der Unfall passiert?
D Warum war Ben erst vor ein paar Wochen im Krankenhaus?
E Wer ist mit Ben ins Krankenhaus gefahren?
F Wer hat den Krankenwagen gerufen?

1b skill: reading TB p. 166

Read the story on page 102 of your textbook again. Answer the questions from 1a in English.

1 ______________________________

2 ______________________________

3 ______________________________

4 ______________________________

5 ______________________________

6 ______________________________

Ben's email

2a grammar in short: 16 simple past

Complete Ben's email to his uncle. Choose a verb from the box and put it in the *simple past*.

call · have · stop · be · want · cry · go · fall · get · hit

New Message

To: uncleleroy@camdenroad.com

Subject: My accident :-(

Hi Uncle Leroy! I'm lying in hospital because I ____________ an accident! I ____________ in Camden with my friends and an e-scooter ____________ me in the leg. I ____________ over and ____________ . The driver ____________ an ambulance for me and I ____________ to hospital. But the worst part is I ____________ a cast for my leg and I have to stay in hospital for a few days. I ____________ to go home yesterday but my mum ____________ me. I ...

2b

Write the end of Ben's email from 2a. Write at least 2 sentences. Use the *simple past*.

The morning rap

3 audio 2/29

Listen to the rap. Circle the things that you hear.

1 

2 

3 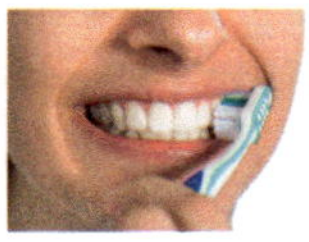

4 

5 

6 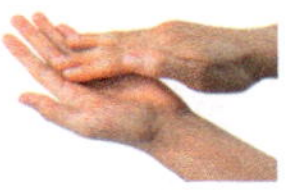

7 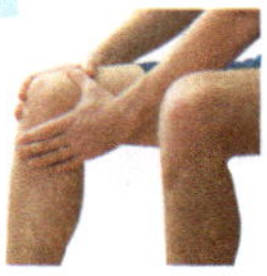

8 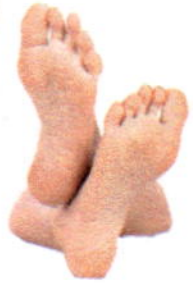

Body parts

4a wordbank: body parts TB p. 190

Write the words next to the right body parts.

arm · back · bottom · ear · eye · face · finger · foot · hair · hand · head · knee · leg · mouth · nose · shoulder · stomach · toe · tooth

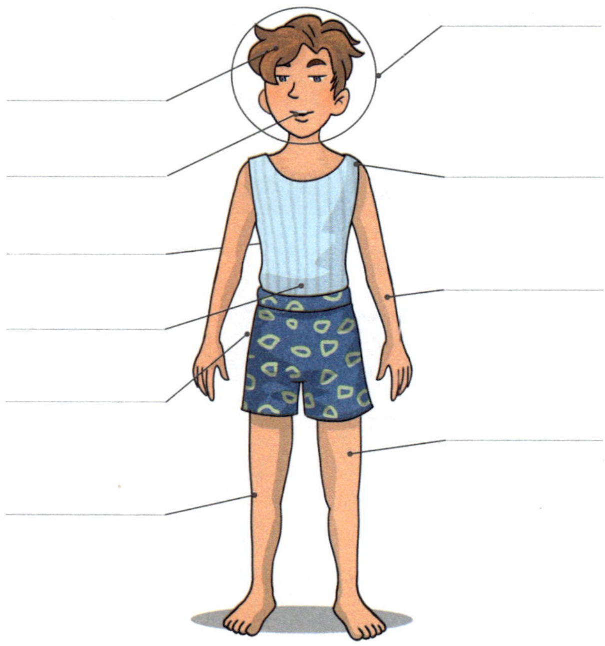

Dusty explains

The nouns *foot* and *tooth* have irregular plural forms. You can look them up in a dictionary.

4b

Look at the body parts in the table. Fill in the plural forms.

one	two or more
hand	*hands*
eye	
ear	
foot	

one	two or more
shoulder	
toe	
tooth	
knee	

Aliens

5a skill: reading TB p. 166

Look at the pictures and then read the texts. Which picture goes with which text?

1

2

3

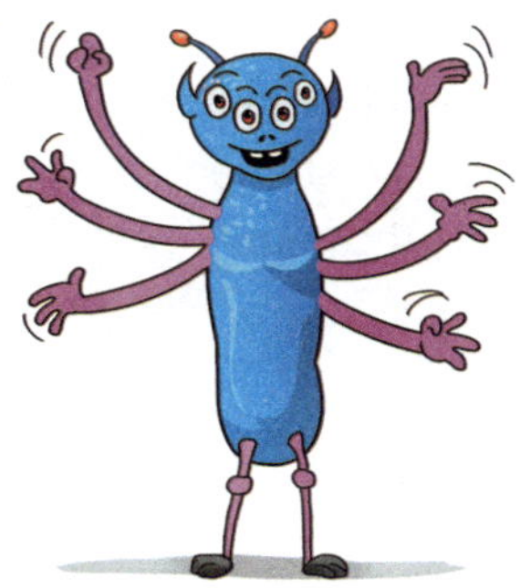

☐ My name is X6AER. I'm from the planet Hagdag. People on Hagdag don't look like people on Earth. I have got four yellow arms. My ears are green and I can hear very well. I have got a small nose. My hair is long and red. Not everyone on Hagdag looks like me. My friend G4DET has got a blue nose and very large feet.

☐ My name is Y2V4. I live on the planet Frof. It is very beautiful. I'm tall and I have got four eyes and six long arms. I go to school every day. I like my school because all my friends go there, too. Some of my friends have got grey bodies and some have got brown bodies and purple arms. But everyone on Frof has got small black feet.

☐ Hi! My name is Bleebleeb. My home is a hot planet very far away. Everyone on my planet has got one eye. I am orange, with big white teeth and three green legs. I like to play football with my friend Klaarg after school. We often go to the cinema, too. We watch films about Earth. I like people from Earth, but I think they look funny!

5b

Read the texts again. Underline all of the body parts. Circle all the colours.

5c

Choose your favourite alien from 5a. Why do you like it? Talk to a partner.

You can say:

I like the first / second / third alien because it is my favourite colour.

It looks funny because it has lots of eyes / arms / …

A group chat

1 skill: reading TB p. 166

Read the conversation between Ben and his friends in your textbook (page 106). Tick (✓) the right answer.

1 How is Ben's leg?

- ☐ It doesn't hurt.
- ☐ It isn't getting better.
- ☐ It still hurts.

2 Who played at the concert?

- ☐ Jack and his friends
- ☐ The Protractors
- ☐ The Barrow Boys

3 Where did Declan get food at the charity concert?

- ☐ from the food trucks
- ☐ from a restaurant
- ☐ from the church

4 How did Ben feel about last night's dinner?

- ☐ not happy
- ☐ disappointed
- ☐ confused

5 Who gets the money from the concert?

- ☐ St Pancras Old Church
- ☐ the animal shelter
- ☐ The Protractors

6 How full was the church?

- ☐ only half full
- ☐ almost full
- ☐ really full

Volunteering

2 skill: mediation TB p. 168

Emmas Bruder Nick sieht dieses Poster und möchte mehr darüber wissen. Bearbeite die Aufgaben stichpunktartig auf Deutsch. Ein Wort genügt nicht.

1 Um wen oder was kümmert sich die RSPCA?

____

2 Was soll man in den zwei Stunden machen?

____

3 Warum sollte man mitmachen?

____

4 Was steht auf dem Poster über Teenager?

____

5 Was steht im Kleingedruckten?

____

____

RSPCA – Working for local animals

WANTED: TWO HOURS OF YOUR TIME!

Can you give out flyers for two hours on a busy street in April and May?

This can help your local RSPCA animal shelter raise money for the animals.

Young teenage volunteers are very welcome!

For a list of RSPCA volunteer locations, go to: www.volunteer.org

Thank you for your support!

A charity registered in England and Wales.

Sound check

3a

Underline all the verbs in the *simple past*.

1 The church opened at 6 p.m.
2 The charity concert started at 7 p.m.
3 Ben really wanted to go to the charity concert.
4 Emma and her brother visited the London Eye.
5 The friends all loved the concert.
6 Emma's brother enjoyed the view of the city.
7 Declan liked the food from the food trucks.
8 Tia talked to her boss after the concert.
9 Emma and her brother walked around London.

3b audio 2/32

Listen to the sentences in 3a. Listen carefully to how the people say *–ed*. Then say the sentences yourself.

3c audio 2/33

Listen to the words and sort them into the table. Then say them yourself.

[ɪd]	[d]	[t]
started	*opened*	*liked*
wanted	*loved*	

wanted · loved · ~~started~~ · walked · jumped · enjoyed · visited · talked · texted · planned · ~~liked~~ · needed · played · ~~opened~~ · completed · arrived · worked · looked

Last weekend

4 skill: writing TB p. 167

Write a short text about what you did last weekend. You can answer the questions.

1 Where did you go?
2 Who did you meet?
3 What did you do or see?
4 What did you like about the activities?

Last weekend, I

4b grammar in short: 16 simple past

What did Emma and her brother do last weekend (✓)? What didn't they do (✗)? Write sentences.

be at a concert (✓) · watch TV (✗) · eat street food (✗) · go to the park (✓) · visit the market (✗) · talk a lot (✓)

1 *Emma and Nick* ______

2 *They* ______

3 ______

4 ______

5 ______

6 ______

Feelings

5a

Read what the friends say and draw their faces. Look at the box for help. Then write down the feelings.

1

It's great that we got a lot of money for the animal shelter!
______

2

I really wanted to go to the concert with my friends, but my leg is broken.
______

3

I want to show my brother all of the cool places in London!
______

4

So many animals still don't have a home and need our help.
______

5

Ugh ... I think I had too much food at the concert.
______

5b

Think about *your* feelings. Answer the questions with one word.

1 What are you happy about? ______

2 What makes you sad? ______

3 What are you worried about? ______

4 What are you excited about? ______

Odd one out

6

Which word is the odd one out? Circle it.

1 hospital | doctor | nurse | animal shelter | ambulance

2 food truck | concert | song | singer | band

3 leg | arm | hand | bed | head

4 morning | evening | last year | night | day

At Camden Market

1

Read the text. Then complete the sentences. Use *can* or *can't* and the verbs in brackets.

You can buy all kinds of clothes at Camden Market: from new and hip to old and second-hand. They sell colourful dresses as well as band shirts, there really is something for everyone. The only clothes they don't sell: touristy souvenir shirts and pullovers. So if you want to bring home a shirt with the King or a hoodie showing Big Ben, look for it somewhere else. If you want to try street food from all over the world or traditional fish and chips, Camden Market is the perfect place. The shops at Camden Market are open from 10am to 8pm daily, even on Sundays.

Everyone ______________ (find) something to wear at Camden Market. You ______________ (buy) touristy shirts at Camden Market, but you ______________ (shop) for new and old things there. You ______________ (eat) at Camden Market, too. They have nice international and traditional English food there. If you think you ______________ (go) shopping at Camden Market on Sundays, you're wrong. The shops are open every day! So you ______________ (come) whenever you want to!

At the doctor

2

Look at the pictures. What's wrong with the patients? What should / shouldn't they do to get better?

0
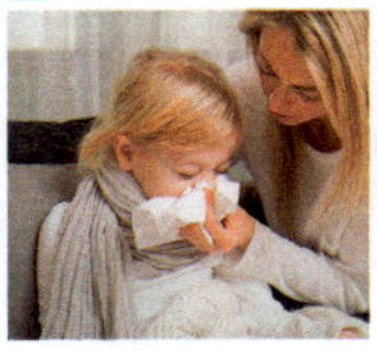
1
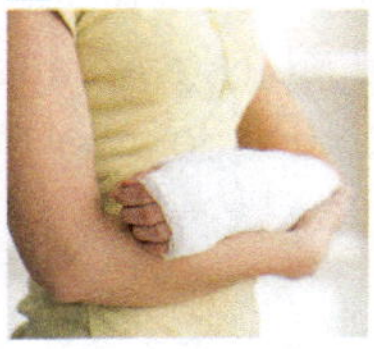
2

3
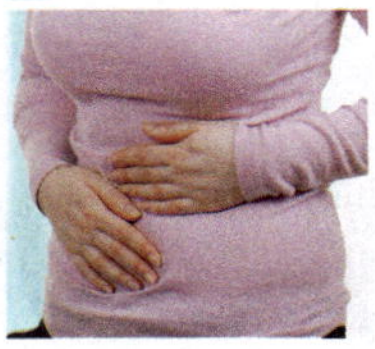
4

5

a toothache · feeling dizzy · ~~a bad cold~~ · a headache · a stomach ache · a broken arm

go to the doctor · stay in bed · sleep a lot · stay at home · drink lots of water · go to school · eat sweets

0 *Patient 0 has a bad cold. She should stay in bed. / She shouldn't go to school.*

1 ______________________________

2 ______________________________

3 ______________________________

4 ______________________________

5 ______________________________

Check out

Speaking solutions p. 84

Talk to a partner. How do the people in the pictures feel? Use the ideas in the box. Take turns.

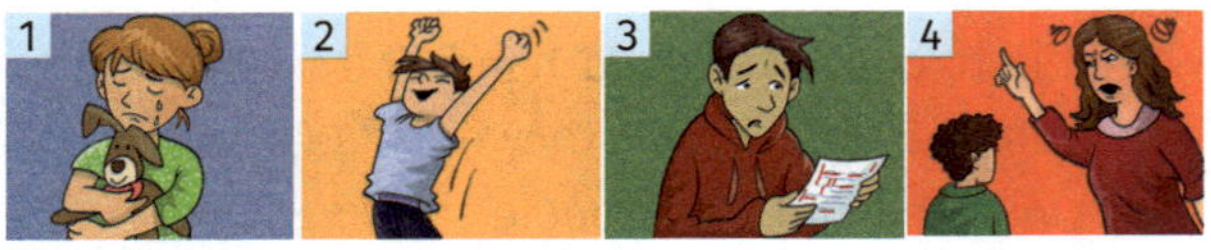

angry · surprised · excited · tired · sad disappointed · happy

You can ask:

How does the girl in picture 1 feel and why? What do you think?

You can answer:

I think she feels sad. Maybe she can't see her friends.

Ich kann: mich über Gefühle unterhalten. ◯

Listening audio 2/38, solutions p. 84

Listen. Find the mistakes and correct them.

0 The weather report is for ~~Scotland~~. England

1 It is cloudy in London.

2 In Birmingham it is hot.

3 Today it is warm and sunny in Manchester.

4 The weather is very cold in York.

Ich kann: einen Wetterbericht verstehen. ◯

Reading solutions p. 84

Read the text and the questions. Underline the answers in the text and write down the right number.

Molly went to the British Museum yesterday (0). She went with her aunt and uncle. They took the bus at 8 a.m. and they arrived at 8.30 a.m. It was great. Tickets are free at the museum so they didn't pay anything to go in. Molly enjoyed learning about history at the museum. After the museum, they went to a burger restaurant and had delicious burgers with chips. It was a great day with her aunt and uncle!

0 When did Molly go to the British Museum?
1 Who did she go with?
2 When did they arrive at the museum?
3 How much do the tickets cost?
4 What did Molly learn about?
5 What did they do after the museum?

Ich kann: einen Text über ein vergangenes Ereignis verstehen. ◯

Writing solutions p. 84

Write about your town. You can use the questions. Write 30-50 words. Use your exercise book.

- What is the name of your town / village?
- What is there in your town / village?
- What is your favourite thing in your town / village?
- What does your town / village not have / offer?
- What is the weather like today?

You can write:

The name of my town is Bamberg. There are many parks and nice cafés. My favourite thing ...

Ich kann: eine Stadt beschreiben. ◯ über das Wetter schreiben. ◯

Mediation solutions p. 84

Lies über Jasmins Wochenende. Bearbeite die Aufgaben stichpunktartig auf Deutsch. Ein Wort genügt nicht.

I had a bad day on Saturday. I met my friends in the park. We played football. It was good fun, but then I fell over. I really hurt my leg. Ouch! My friend called my mum. She came in her car and took me to the hospital. We were in the hospital for about two hours. Then we went home. I slept a lot and I watched TV. It was so boring. I am feeling a little better now, but I still feel sad about my leg. I hope I can go back to school next week ...

1 Was hat Jasmin am Samstag gespielt?

______

2 Was ist dabei passiert?

______

3 Wo ist sie mit ihrer Mutter hingefahren?

______

4 Wie fand sie es, viel zu schlafen und fern zu schauen?

______

5 Wie geht es ihr jetzt?

______

Ich kann: ein vergangenes Ereignis verstehen. ◯

USE OF ENGLISH

Grammar solutions p. 84

Unscramble the questions. Then match them with the answers (A-D). Write down the right numbers.

1 you – go – Where – yesterday – did – ?

______

2 did – What – eat – you – ?

______

3 dessert – you – Did – have – ?

______

4 you – Who – go – did – with ?

______

A I went with my parents. ☐

B I went to a restaurant. ☐

C I ate fish and chips. ☐

D No, I didn't. ☐

Vocabulary solutions p. 84

Underline the odd word out and think of a suitable word for each line.

1 cinema – park – cricket – shop ______

2 blue – arm – eye – hand ______

3 sunny – rainy – cloudy – charity ______

4 angry – happy – sad – worried ______

Ich kann: nach Dingen in der Vergangenheit fragen. ◯

Holiday activities at home

1a wordbank: holidays TB p. 191

Find twelve more holiday words.

b	a	s	h	f	u	h	l	v	o	l	l	e	y	b	a	l	l	b	b
i	t	h	e	p	l	i	c	o	r	e	a	d	o	r	d	f	s	d	k
c	h	m	b	i	k	k	g	l	w	c	i	n	e	m	a	s	l	n	k
k	l	u	b	i	k	e	z	e	y	e	t	b	l	m	c	o	o	k	o
f	e	s	p	i	s	o	i	y	j	r	p	i	x	a	p	d	e	h	s
i	t	i	e	s	h	o	r	a	e	d	t	h	g	h	a	q	p	d	w
l	i	c	k	u	c	l	e	s	s	u	i	n	g	m	r	u	g	s	i
m	c	d	r	o	m	s	a	m	u	b	e	c	l	a	k	e	l	d	m
g	s	a	i	l	y	o	g	a	t	u	m	u	s	e	u	m	d	m	u

1b

Choose 6 of the words you found in 1a. Write sentences.

0 *I watched a new film with my friends at the weekend.*

1 ____________________

2 ____________________

3 ____________________

4 ____________________

5 ____________________

6 ____________________

Lisa and Holly's holidays

2a skill: reading TB p. 166

Read what Lisa says about holidays. Highlight the weather words in yellow and the activities in blue.

Holidays are great! I can stay up late and get up late. On warm and sunny days, I go swimming. I also enjoy riding my bike and meeting my friends. I love going camping with my mum. We really like places like Wales and Scotland. On cold or rainy days, we visit sights like castles or museums. And when the weather is nice, we go hiking or play volleyball.

2b audio 2/42, skill: listening TB p. 165

Now listen to Holly. Write down all the words for weather and name at least three activities.

weather words: ____________________

____

activities: ____________________

____

2c audio 2/42, skill: listening TB p. 165

What do Lisa and Holly do in what weather? Read the text in 2a again and listen to Holly again. Complete the table.

on warm and sunny days	on cold and rainy days	in all types of weather

At the skate park

3 skill: mediation TB p. 168

Sams deutsche Cousine (12) versteht das Schild im Skatepark nicht. Bearbeite die Aufgaben stichpunktartig auf Deutsch. Ein Wort genügt nicht.

SOUTHWELL SKATE PARK RULES

- Skateboards, inline skates and scooters only.
- Don't ride your bicycle in the park.
- You must wear a helmet if you are under 16.
- You should wear knee pads, elbow pads and wrist guards.
- Don't bring any glass containers into the park.
- Please keep the park clean.
- Park closed from dusk to dawn.

Skate at your own risk!

1 Kann ich hier mein Fahrrad benutzen?

____

____

2 Muss ich einen Helm tragen?

____

3 Was ist im Skate Park verboten?

____

4 Wann macht der Park zu?

____

Orla's dream holiday

4 grammar in short: 18 imperative

Orla dreams about her perfect holiday at home. Write down what the other people should or should not do.

0 Grandparents: *Please go to the cinema with me and buy me lots of popcorn.*

1 Parents: ______________________

____

2 Friends: ______________________

____

3 Parents: ______________________

____

4 Friends: ______________________

____

5 Little brother: ______________________

____

Where are you going this summer?

1 audio 2/46, skill: listening TB p. 165

Listen to the interview and tick (✓) the right answers.

1 Who is Sam visiting in Cornwall?

- [ ] his grandpa
- [ ] his grandma
- [ ] his friend Edward

2 What do he and his sister want to do in Cornwall?

- [ ] eat lots of ice cream
- [ ] go diving
- [ ] visit museums

3 Where is Harry going on Monday?

- [ ] to the beach
- [ ] on a boat tour.
- [ ] to museums

4 Why does Sofia's family stay at home?

- [ ] They don't have time to go away.
- [ ] It is cheap.
- [ ] They live in a beautiful city.

5 What does Sofia like about her holiday?

- [ ] She goes to an expensive hotel.
- [ ] She eats yummy food at nice restaurants.
- [ ] She can sleep in her own bed.

6 What are Jordan's plans for his stay in Cardiff?

- [ ] eating and hiking
- [ ] swimming and diving
- [ ] shopping and sightseeing

Cornish Adventure Camp

2 skill: mediation TB p. 168

Du möchtest im Sommer ins Cornish Adventure Camp. Beantworte die Fragen deiner Mutter stichpunktartig auf Deutsch. Ein Wort genügt nicht.

There is never a boring moment at the Cornish Adventure Camp in the beautiful town of Newquay.

Newquay has some of the **best beaches** in the UK. We do lots of fun activities at the beach like **bodyboarding** and **surfing**. We also go on a treasure hunt to explore the town.

When it's rainy, you can come with us to **Blue Reef Newquay.** It's an amazing aquarium with an underwater tunnel.

So don't miss out and spend your holidays at the Cornish Adventure Camp!

Two travel periods:
28th July – 4th August
14th August – 21st August
9 to 14 years: £369
15 to 18 years: £399

1 Wo genau ist das Camp?

____

2 Was könnt ihr dort machen?

____

____

3 Was ist, wenn das Wetter schlecht ist?

____

4 Wann findet das Camp statt?

____

5 Was kostet das Camp, wenn auch dein 16-jähriger Cousin mitfährt?

____

A postcard from Wales

3 grammar in short: 14 word order in statements

Complete the postcard with *and*, *or*, *but* or *because*.

12th August

Dear Rishi,

Wales is a cool place! Yesterday we visited a famous castle ____________ today we went to the top of Mount Snowdon. Mum and I walked for four hours ____________ Dad and Sarah only needed one hour ____________ they took the Snowdon Mountain Railway. We were really lucky ____________ we had no clouds ____________ rain ____________ we had a great view from the top. Tomorrow we are going to the beach ____________ we are visiting a museum – we must see what the weather is like.

Love,
Grace

Rishi Patel
49 Fitzroy Road
London
NW1 8TP
United Kingdom

Holiday plans

4a

Lisa is looking forward to her holidays. She's writing in her diary about her plans. Put the verbs in brackets in the *present progressive* and fill in the gaps.

Dear diary,

On Sunday we ____________________ **(go)** on holiday to Scotland. We ____________________ **(stay)** in a caravan near Inverness. I want to do so many things. On Monday I ____________________ **(visit)** the children's edutainment centre at the Loch Ness Centre and my parents ____________________ **(get)** tickets for a Loch Ness cruise. I hope I can see Nessie! On Tuesday we ____________________ **(drive)** to the Highlands. Dad ____________________ **(hike)** up Ben Nevis, and Mum and I ____________________ **(have)** a cup of tea and ____________________ **(walk)** around a bit. On Friday we ____________________ **(go)** back home. I'm looking forward to seeing my friends again!

4b

What is Lisa packing for her holidays in Scotland? Write down the words.

1 ˈsʌnˌglɑːsɪz	______	4 ˈtaʊəl	______
2 ˈfəʊn	______	5 ˈpʊləʊvə	______
3 ˈtraʊzəz	______	6 ˈdaɪəri	______

4c skill: working with words TB p. 162

Write down twelve things you pack for a holiday in a city or at the beach. Look up words you don't know.

______ ______ ______

______ ______ ______

______ ______ ______

______ ______ ______

On the way

5 skill: working with words TB p. 164, wordbank: travelling TB p. 183

Match the means of transport and the right verb. Then write sentences.

Ben and Declan – to the pool	Lisa's family – to Scotland	Mr Smith – to work	Tia – to Cyprus	Declan – to Brighton
1 	2 	3 	4 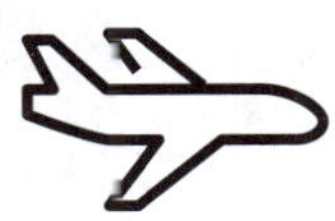	5 
fly	go	ride	drive	go

1 *Ben and Declan ride to the pool by bike.*

2 ______

3 ______

4 ______

5 ______

What's happening?

1 skill: describing pictures TB p. 172

Read the text on pages 126 / 127 in your textbook again and put the pictures in the right order. Then write what is happening in each picture.

☐ 

☐ 

☐ 

☐ 

☐ 

☐ 

☐ 

1 

The four friends are walking on the beach.

On the beach

2a
skill: working with words TB p. 164 + describing pictures TB p. 172

Describe the picture and look up the words you don't know in a dictionary.

2b

Describe the picture. Write about 50 words.

In the picture I can see

Getting information abroad

3

You are on holiday. What can you ask in English when you want to know the following things?

1 ... wann und wo es Frühstück gibt.

2 ... wie du zum Strand kommst.

3 ... wo die nächste Bushaltestelle ist.

4 ... was die Postkarten und eine Briefmarke nach Deutschland kosten.

Weather poems

4 skill: writing TB p. 167

Read the weather poems. Then write your weather poem. You can collect ideas in a word web first.

Sunday, Sunday,
Can we have some sun today?
I want a sunny Sunday!
Oh, here's the rain ...

rain
and clouds
books and games
a summer day in England

Packing my suitcase

5

Sort the words from the box into the right suitcase. Some words fit into more than one suitcase. Add more words.

hiking sticks · scarf · gloves · sunglasses · raincoat · surfboard · hiking boots · cap · T-shirt · shorts · winter hat · pullover · coat · sunscreen · swimsuit · goggles · snowboard

1) summer holidays in Spain **2) outdoor holidays in Sweden** **3) winter holidays in Austria**

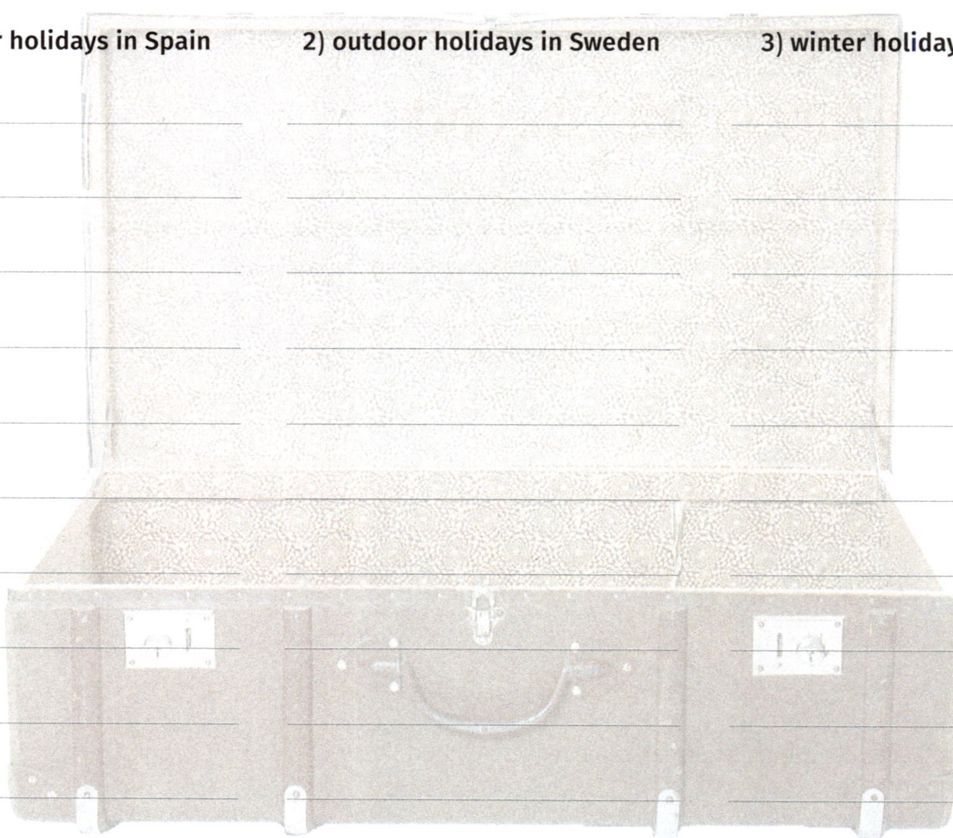

Visiting Germany

1a skill: reading TB p. 166

In the summer holidays Tia's friend June went to Germany with her parents.
Read her holiday diary. What did she like about her holiday in Germany? Underline in the text.

Saturday, 8th August

Today I arrived in Nuremberg. We needed fourteen hours by car to get here. The ride was so boring!
We are staying with my aunt and her family. They have a small flat in the city centre.
After a small snack we wanted to go for a walk and see Nuremberg by night, but it started to rain and we had to stay inside.
We sat in the living room and played board games. Not my thing … but everyone else had fun. So after a while I went to the kitchen with my phone and chatted with my friends. I miss them already … I wish I could be with them now. I'm feeling really sad and lonely.

Sunday, 9th August

In the morning it was sunny and dry. We took the tram and then walked to the "Kaiserburg", a big castle in the middle of the city. You have a great view over Nuremberg from it. My cousin came with us. He is thirteen and so nice! After that we bought some "Nürnberger Lebkuchen". It's actually a christmas treat but in Nuremberg you can buy it all year round. Yummy!
In the afternoon we went to the zoo. There weren't any elephants, but I loved the beautiful tigers.
Now I'm really tired. I wasn't sad today.
I was really happy. It was a wonderful day!

1b

Put the sentences in the right order.

- ☐ June was bored and went to the kitchen.
- ☐ After the walk they bought a speciality from Nuremberg.
- ☐ June arrived in Nuremberg on Saturday.
- ☐ Then they went to the zoo.
- ☐ They stayed inside and played board games.
- ☐ On Sunday morning they visited a castle.

1c skill: writing TB p. 167

Write a diary entry about a fantastic or a boring day during your holidays. Think about activities, the weather and how you got to different places.

Check out

Speaking solutions p. 85

Talk to a partner. Choose a picture. Say what you see and when you use it. Take turns.

1 
2 
3 
4 
5 
6 

You can say:

I picture 1 I can see a bus.
I take the bus to school every day.
What about you?

Ich kann: über Verkehrsmittel sprechen. ◯

Listening audio 2/53, solutions p. 85

Listen. Find the right order of the pictures (A-E).

Ich kann: verstehen, was andere (nicht) tun sollen. ◯

Mediation solutions p. 85

Lies, was Tom und Pippa sagen. Bearbeite die Aufgaben stichpunktartig auf Deutsch. Ein Wort genügt nicht.

Tom: Pippa, what are you doing at the weekend?
Pippa: I am going shopping with my sister. Why?
Tom: Nice! My friends and I are going to the seaside. Maybe you would like to come, too?
Pippa: Oh, that sounds fun. Yes, sure. When are you going?
Tom: We are going on Saturday. We're taking the tram at 2 p.m.
Pippa: Great. My sister and I are going shopping at 10 a.m., so 2 p.m. is fine. Are you going somewhere for lunch?
Tom: No, we are eating before we leave.
Pippa: Ok. Let's meet at the tram stop at 1.50 p.m. then ...

1 Was hat Pippa am Wochenende vor?

2 Was machen Tom und seine Freunde?

3 Wann wollen alle zusammen losfahren?

Ich kann: Pläne für die nähere Zukunft verstehen. ◯

Writing solutions p. 85

Write a text about your plans for holidays at home. You can use the questions. Write 30-50 words.

- What are you doing?
- Where are you going?
- Who are you meeting?

You can write:

In the holidays I am meeting my cousin in the park. We are playing table tennis together. I am going swimming with my mum, too ...

Ich kann: über Ferien zu Hause schreiben. ◯

Reading solutions p. 85

a) Read the text and tick (✓) the sentence which summarises the text best.

Spend a great family weekend in Blackpool!

Blackpool is a city in the north-west of England. There are lots of things to do: You can visit Blackpool Zoo and see some beautiful animals like tigers and elephants. You can enjoy the many cafés on the seaside and eat some tasty fish and chips. Or why not go to the beach and swim in the sea? There are also lots of interesting museums like Madame Tussauds. And don't forget about Blackpool Pleasure Beach: a big amusement park at the seaside!

- ☐ The text is about a special tiger and elephant.
- ☐ The text is about a holiday destination in England.
- ☐ The text is about means of transport in Blackpool.

b) Answer the questions. You do not have to write complete sentences.

1 Where is Blackpool? __________

2 What animals can you find at Blackpool Zoo? __________

3 What food can you eat at Blackpool? __________

4 What is Madame Tussauds? __________

5 What is Blackpool Pleasure Beach? __________

Ich kann: einen Text über einen typischen Urlaubsort in Großbritannien verstehen. ◯

USE OF ENGLISH

Grammar solutions p. 85

What are they planning to do tomorrow? Write sentences with the phrases from the box.

0 
1 
2 
3 
4 

go abroad · bake a cake · walk the dog · ~~visit her grandma~~ · clean the room

0 *She is visiting her grandma.*

1 __________

2 __________

3 __________

4 __________

Vocabulary solutions p. 85

Underline words or expressions in the text that mean the same as the expressions on the right.

Next week, my family and I are going abroad (0). We are travelling by plane to Italy. I am so excited! We are meeting my aunt, uncle and cousins there. We are staying in a hotel. At the hotel, there is a big swimming pool. We are swimming all day. I hope the weather is hot and sunny! We are taking our sunglasses and shorts. In the evenings, we are going to different restaurants to try lots of different food like pizza and pasta. Oh, and ice cream, of course!

0 in another country
1 flying
2 your mum or dad's brother
3 the opposite of cold
4 trousers you wear when it's hot
5 a cold dessert

Ich kann: Pläne für die nähere Zukunft ausdrücken. ◯ einen Text zu Urlaubsorten im Ausland verstehen. ◯

Check out – Unit 1

Speaking & Writing

Individuelle Lösungen

Mediation

Lies, was Zoe sagt. Beschreibe ihren Bruder stichpunktartig auf Deutsch. Ein Wort genügt nicht.

Beispiellösung:

Zoes Bruder heißt Jack. Er ist 13 Jahre alt und er wohnt mit Zoe und ihren Eltern in London. Seine Lieblingsfarbe ist rot. Er hat eine rote Gitarre und er liebt Musik.

Reading

Read the sentences and tick (✓) them right, wrong or not in the text.

1	Dylan is 11 years old.	**right**
2	His dream room is small.	**wrong**
3	It has got one bed.	**wrong**
4	There is a computer.	**right**
5	He has got a sister.	**not in the text**
6	He plays video games every day.	**not in the text**

Listening

Read what Zoe says. Describe her brother in German.

FACT FILE
Name: Jonas
Age: 11
Place: Regensburg
Brothers / Sisters: two sisters
Pets: no pets

Grammar

Fill in the correct *possessive pronouns*.

1 my
2 His
3 our
4 my
5 my aunt's / her
6 Her
7 my aunt and uncle's / their
8 my uncle's / his

Vocabulary

Write down the missing words.

1 Germany
2 small
3 house
4 parents
5 yellow
6 bed
7 desk
8 On
9 desk
10 lamp
11 books
12 TV
13 computer

Check out – Unit 2

Speaking & Writing

Individuelle Lösungen

Listening

Listen to Olivia. Write short answers to the questions (1-5).

1 five
2 ICT
3 because she has PE early in the morning
4 French and ICT
5 RE

Reading

Read the sentences and tick (✓) them right, wrong or not in the text.

1	Jasmin is Sam's sister.	**right**
2	They eat different breakfasts.	**wrong**
3	Sam usually drinks milk.	**wrong**
4	Sometimes Sam eats an. apple, too	**right**
5	Sam eats cereal every day.	**wrong**
6	He plays video games every day.	**not in the text**
7	Jasmin loves Sundays.	**not in the text**

Mediation

Lies, was die Lehrkraft sagt. Bearbeite die Aufgaben stichpunktartig auf Deutsch. Ein Wort genügt nicht.

1 einen Mathethest
2 einen schwarzen Stift, einen Bleistift und ein Lineal. Ein Radiergummi ist auch eine gute Idee.
3 Papier
4 einen blauen Stift
5 um 10 Uhr
6 pünktlich anzukommen

Grammar

Read the sentences and write down the negatives.

1 Mrs Newton doesn't teach science.
2 We haven't got ten books.
3 Our school isn't in France.
4 I don't read a book every day.
5 He can't play football.
6 They don't like maths.

Vocabulary

Read the sentences and write down the negatives.

1 fried egg
2 sausages
3 toast
4 butter
5 jam
6 tea
7 milk
8 orange juice

Check out – Unit 3

Speaking & Writing

Individuelle Lösungen

Mediation

Schaue dir das Poster an. Bearbeite die Aufgaben stichpunktartig auf Deutsch. Ein Wort genügt nicht.

1 am 30. Oktober in der Schule
2 alle Schülerinnen und Schüler
3 zwei Pfund
4 Würste (auch vegetarisch) und Burgers, sowie Pfannkuchen und Schokolade als Nachtisch

Reading

Read the sentences and tick (✓) them right, wrong or not in the text.

1 Robin is celebrating her birthday.	**right**
2 Her brother is eating lots of crisps.	**wrong**
3 Her aunt and uncle are playing games.	**right**
4 Robin is dancing with her friends.	**right**
5 Robin's grandpa is at the party, too.	**not in the text**

Listening

Listen. Find the right order of the pictures. Be careful, there are more pictures than you need.

Grammar

a) What is Chloe doing? Write down short answers.

1 No, she isn't.
2 Yes, she is.
3 No, she isn't.
4 No, they aren't.

b) Use the correct form of the verbs in the box.

1 is reading
2 is drinking
3 is writing
4 am doing

Vocabulary

Read the sentences and tick (✓) them right, wrong or not in the text.

1 ~~his~~ is
2 ~~bad~~ cool
3 ~~When~~ how
4 ~~They~~ There

Check out – Unit 4

Speaking & Writing

Individuelle Lösungen

Listening

Listen to Michael. Tick (✓) the three sports he likes doing.

Michael likes: tennis, field hockey, cricket

Reading

Where do these sentences fit in the text? Find the best place and write the letters A, B, C, D, E or F in the box. Be careful, there are more letters than you need.

Let me tell you about my friends. Annabel loves cooking. She cooks every weekend. [C] Will enjoys playing football. [F] Chrissie is a very quiet person. She likes sitting in her bedroom and reading. [A] My brother is a very loud person. He loves music. [E] Oh, and what about me? Well, I am a creative person. [B] What is your hobby?

Mediation

Lies, was Ines sagt. Vervollständige die Tabelle stichpunktartig auf Deutsch. Ein Wort genügt nicht.

Wer?	Was macht er / sie regelmäßig?	Was macht er / sie gerade?
Ines	*Hausaufgaben / Musik hören*	*fernsehen*
ihr Bruder	*zum Park gehen / Fußball spielen*	*einen Freund besuchen / Computerspiele spielen*
ihre Schwester	*Tennistraining*	*schlafen*

Grammar

Read the text. Rank Mia's activities from 1 (most often) to 5 (never).

5  4  1 

2  3 

Vocabulary

Write down the missing words.

1 horse
2 chickens
3 cat
4 goat
5 cows
6 dog

Check out – Unit 5

Speaking & Writing

Individuelle Lösungen

Listening

Listen. Find the mistakes and correct them.

1 ~~cloudy~~ – sunny
2 ~~hot~~ – cold / cloudy
3 ~~warm and sunny~~ – rainy
4 ~~cold~~ – hot

Reading

Read the text and the questions. Underline the answers in the text and write down the correct number.

Molly went to the British Museum (0) yesterday. She went with (1) her aunt and uncle. They took the bus at 8 a.m. and they arrived (2) at 8.30 a.m. It was great. (3) Tickets are free at the museum so they didn't pay anything to go in. Molly enjoyed learning about (4) history at the museum. After the museum, (5) they went to a burger restaurant and had delicious burgers with chips. It was a great day with her aunt and uncle!

Mediation

Lies über Jasmins Wochenende. Bearbeite die Aufgaben stichpunktartig auf Deutsch. Ein Wort genügt nicht.

1 Fußball
2 Sie ist umgefallen.
3 ins Krankenhaus
4 langweilig
5 ein bisschen besser / sie ist traurig wegen ihres Beines

Grammar

Read what Jasmin says. Answer the questions in German.

1 Where did you go yesterday?
2 What did you eat?
3 Did you have dessert?
4 Who did you go with?

A I went with my parents. 4
B I went to a restaurant. 1
C I ate fish and chips. 2
D No, I didn't. 3

Vocabulary

Read what Jasmin says. Answer the questions in German.

Beispiellösung:

1 cricket – school
2 blue – leg
3 charity – windy
4 happy – nervous

Check out – Unit 6

Speaking & Writing

Individuelle Lösungen

Listening

Listen. Find the right order of the pictures (A-E).

2

3

1

4

5

Mediation

Lies, was Tom und Pippa sagen. Bearbeite die Aufgaben stichpunktartig auf Deutsch. Ein Wort genügt nicht.

1 Sie geht mit ihrer Schwester shoppen.
2 Sie fahren ans Meer.
3 um 14 Uhr

Grammar

What are they planning to do tomorrow? Write sentences with the phrases from the box.

1 He is cleaning the room.
2 They are baking a cake.
3 They are going abroad.
4 She is walking the dog.

Reading

a) Read the text and tick (✓) the sentence which summarises the text best.

✓ The text is about a holiday destination in England.

b) Answer the questions. You do not have to write complete sentences.

1 in the north-west of England
2 tigers and elephants
3 fish and chips
4 a museum
5 a big amusement park

Vocabulary

Underline words or expressions in the text that mean the same as the expressions on the right.

Next week, my family and I are going [0] abroad. We are [1] travelling by plane to Italy. I am so excited! We are meeting my aunt, [2] uncle and cousins there. We are staying in a hotel. At the hotel, there is a big swimming pool. We are swimming all day. I hope the weather is [3] hot and sunny! We are taking our sunglasses and [4] shorts. In the evenings, we are going to different restaurants to try lots of different food like pizza and pasta. Oh, and [5] ice cream, of course

Audiotracks

Welcome
1/1 **TB 1b** Camden Road
1/2 **TB 2a** Colours
1/3 **TB 3a** Numbers
1/4 **TB 3b** Numbers
1/5 **WB 2b** 1, 2, 3, ...
1/6 **TB 4a** The alphabet
1/7 **WB 4** The alphabet
1/8 **TB 5a** My name is ...
1/9 **TB 5c** My name is ...
1/10 **WB 5a** New in Camden

Unit 1 – Part A
1/11 **TB 1b** Check in – Meet Tia
1/12 **TB 1** About Tia
1/13 **WB 2** Sound check
1/14 **TB 2a** Where are you from?
1/15 **TB 2c** Where are you from?
1/16 **TB 3a** A text message

Unit 1 – Part B
1/17 **TB 1a** Our pets
1/18 **TB 3** The dragon
1/19 **TB 4a** All kinds of pets

Unit 1 – Part C
1/20 **TB 1b** Visiting Emma
1/21 **TB 2a/2b** Emma's family
1/22 **TB 4a** Dream room
1/23 **WB 4** Tom's blue bed
1/24 **WB 6a** Megan's family tree
1/25 **TB** Check out – Listening
1/26 **TB** Check out – Mediation
1/27 **TB** Check out – Reading
1/28 **WB** Check out – Listening

Unit 2 – Part A
1/29 **TB 1b** Check in – At Haverstock School
1/30 **TB 2a** Check in – Two friends at school
1/31 **TB 2b** Check in –Two friends at school
1/32 **TB 2** Right or wrong?
1/33 **TB 6** Classroom phrases
1/34 **WB 2** More classroom phrases
1/35 **WB 3b** Ready for school

Unit 2 – Part B
1/36 **TB 1a** New friends at school
1/37 **TB 2a** More about Haverstock School
1/38 **TB 2b** More about Haverstock School
1/39 **TB 3** Lots of clubs at Haverstock School
1/40 **WB 1** A day at Haverstock School
1/41 **TB 6a** Days of the week
1/42 **TB 8b** What they don't do

Unit 2 – Part C
1/43 **TB 1b** Emma's crazy morning
1/44 **TB 2a** Ways to school
1/45 **TB 3a** Emma's breakfast
1/46 **WB 6** Sound check
1/47 **TB 3b** Culture – Schools in Great Britain
1/48 **TB** Check out – Listening
1/49 **TB** Check out – Mediation
1/50 **TB** Check out – Reading
1/51 **WB** Check out – Listening

Unit 3 – Part A
1/52 **TB 1b** Check in – Festivals
1/53 **TB 1b** Preparations
1/54 **TB 3a** Facts about Diwali
1/55 **TB 4a** Pancake Day
1/56 **TB 6b** What are you doing?

Unit 3 – Part B
1/57 **TB 1a** Party preparations
1/58 **TB 2a** Shopping for the party
1/59 **TB 2b** Shopping for the party
1/60 **TB 3c** Bingo
1/61 **TB 3d** Bingo
1/62 **WB 4** Sound check

Unit 3 – Part C
2/1 **TB 1b** Tia's birthday party
2/2 **TB 2** Dusty's birthday invitation
2/3 **TB 4a** The Hendersons' birthday calendar
2/4 **TB 2** Culture – Festivals in the UK
2/5 **TB** Check out – Mediation
2/6 **TB** Check out – Listening
2/7 **TB** Check out – Reading
2/8 **WB** Check out – Listening

Unit 4 – Part A
2/9 **TB 1b** Check in – Hobbies and activities
2/10 **TB 1a** Clubs at Camden Youth Club
2/11 **TB 1c** Clubs at Camden Youth Club
2/12 **TB 5** An interview

Unit 4 – Part B
2/13 **TB 1b** What a terrible day!
2/14 **WB 2** During the match

Unit 4 – Part C
2/15 **TB 1b** A day at the farm
2/16 **WB 3b/3c** Farm photos
2/17 **TB 2** Junior farmer for a day
2/18 **TB** Check out – Mediation
2/19 **TB** Check out – Listening
2/20 **TB** Check out – Reading
2/21 **WB** Check out – Listening

Unit 5 – Part A
2/22 **TB 1b** Check in – What is happening?
2/23 **TB 1a** Around Camden
2/24 **TB 3a/3b** More places in Camden
2/25 **WB 3** A lot to do in Camden
2/26 **TB 11** Weather around the world

Unit 5 – Part B
2/27 **TB 1b** Poor Ben
2/28 **TB 3** A charity concert
2/29 **WB 3** The morning rap

Unit 5 – Part C
2/30 **TB 1a** A charity concert
2/31 **TB 1d** A charity concert
2/32 **WB 3b** Sound check
2/33 **WB 3c** Sound check
2/34 **TB 1b** Culture – London sights
2/35 **TB** Check out – Mediation
2/36 **TB** Check out – Reading
2/37 **TB** Check out – Listening
2/38 **WB** Check out – Listening

Unit 6 – Part A
2/39 **TB 1a/1b** Check in – My holidays
2/40 **TB 1b** Holidays at home
2/41 **TB 2** Holidays are great

2/42 **WB 2b/2c** Lisa and Holly's holidays
2/43 **TB 4a** Meeting @ the pool
2/44 **TB 5a** A holiday song

Unit 6 – Part B
2/45 **TB 1a** Holiday tips
2/46 **WB 1** Where are you going this summer?
2/47 **TB 3a** Places around Britain

Unit 6 – Part C
2/48 **TB 1b** On the beach in Cyprus
2/49 **TB 4a** Weather in Europe

2/50 **TB** Check out – Listening
2/51 **TB** Check out – Mediation
2/52 **TB** Check out – Reading
2/53 **WB** Check out – Listening

Story
2/54 Blaze and the Edinburgh Dragons 1
2/55 Blaze and the Edinburgh Dragons 2
2/56 Blaze and the Edinburgh Dragons 3

Audios

Tonstudio: 2020 Recordings, London; Directed by Stefan Szwarc, Sound Design by Jack Hutchings und TEFL Audio, London; Produzenten: John Green, Tim Woolf.
Gesprochen von: Luke Francis, Emily Joyce, Helen Keeley, Evie Mitchell, Dray Oli, Nathaniel Priestley, Zane Siddiqui, Ellis Sutherland, Maya Thomas and Sofia Thomas.
Songs:
CD 1: 6: The alphabet © Bildungshaus Schulbuchverlage GmbH, Braunschweig. Lyrics Kathrin Müller, Kirkintilloch, music Tobias Friedrich, Berlin.
CD 2: 44: A holiday song: © Bildungshaus Schulbuchverlage GmbH, Braunschweig. Lyrics Amy Frances Koerner, Portsmouth, music Tim Woolf, London.

Bildquellen

|Alamy Stock Photo, Abingdon/Oxfordshire: Cooper, Noriko 32.9; Evans, Robert 60.7; Johnson, Roy 33.1, 33.2; LEE SNIDER 32.3; Xtremer 43.9. |Alamy Stock Photo (RMB), Abingdon/Oxfordshire: Allred, Nathan 39.57; Deioma, Kayte 28.1; Einsiedel, Andreas von 51.4; Honcharuk, Valerii 37.8; JGI/Jamie Grill / Blend Images 32.12; jupiter8 13.2; Melting Spot 32.7; Morley, Caroline 51.3; Oberhäuser, Rupert 51.6; Rann, Kelly 37.5; razorpix 35.4, 35.5; Saunderson, Johnny 17.1, 17.2; Tim Gainey 35.11. |Art Explosion, Calabasas, CA: 9.3, 19.3. |Ellert, Mario, Bremen: 50.1, 61.1, 111.1. |fotolia.com, New York: absolutimages 65.4, 65.10; adamgolabak 9.4; Alexander Raths 67.1; Herrndorff 78.1, 85.1, 85.1; Irochka 39.59, 39.60; Mainka, Markus 79.5; marino 37.4; Monkey Business 32.10; moonrun 9.2; robynmac 31.1; Smileus 32.11; Tim UR 35.9; Tobias Arhelger (Wurst) 31.2; VadimGuzhva 65.2, 65.8; viperagp 31.8. |Getty Images (RF), München: FatCamera 85.3; Krinke, Michael 85.2; Robert Pickett 51.2. |iStockphoto.com, Calgary: alvarez 39.46; andresr 79.4; bazilfoto 50.3; bergamont 27.2, 35.6; Boarding1Now 27.4, 31.9; Brainsil 32.8; biriemoments 51.5; Burt, Samuel 31.6, 31.7; Dmytro Leshchenko 50.2; FatCamera 42.3, 78.6, 85.3; Fertnig 79.1; GlobalP 39.49, 55.6, 55.7, 55.11; hadynyah 68.1; HelenaQueen 31.3, 31.4; Krinke, Michael 78.2, 85.2; Leonsbox 55.8; loops7 10.1; maxoidos 10.2; mejnak 4.6, 4.7; PeopleImages 60.3; Putrisetya163 54.5; Ranta Images 32.2; RuslanDashinsky 39.58; santypan 32.13; SeventyFour 37.1; tetmc 39.45; Wavebreakmedia 62.1; yuliya 35.1, 35.2, 42.7; zeleno 27.6. |juniors@wildlife Bildagentur GmbH, Hamburg: Giel, O. 11.1. |Marckwort, Ulf, Kassel: 11.10, 40.1, 56.1, 56.3, 61.3, 61.4, 61.5, 66.1, 66.3, 66.5, 66.7, 66.8. |Naumann, Andrea, Aachen: 4.3, 5.1, 5.1, 5.2, 5.2, 5.3, 5.3, 5.4, 5.4, 5.5, 5.6, 5.6, 5.7, 5.7, 5.8, 5.8, 5.9, 5.9, 5.10, 5.10, 5.11, 5.11, 6.1, 8.1, 11.7, 11.8, 11.9, 12.2, 12.3, 12.4, 12.5, 14.1, 14.2, 15.1, 15.2, 15.3, 15.4, 15.5, 15.6, 15.7, 16.1, 16.2, 16.3, 16.4, 16.5, 16.6, 16.7, 16.8, 16.9, 19.2, 19.5, 19.6, 19.7, 19.8, 19.9, 19.10, 19.11, 21.1, 21.2, 21.3, 21.4, 22.1, 22.2, 22.3, 24.1, 24.1, 24.2, 24.2, 24.3, 24.3, 24.4, 24.5, 24.6, 24.6, 24.7, 24.8, 24.9, 24.10, 24.11, 24.12, 24.13, 24.14, 24.15, 24.16, 27.7, 27.8, 27.9, 27.10, 27.11, 30.1, 30.2, 32.1, 34.1, 37.9, 38.1, 38.2, 38.3, 38.4, 38.5, 38.6, 38.7, 38.8, 38.9, 38.10, 38.11, 38.12, 38.13, 38.14, 38.15, 38.15, 38.16, 39.1, 39.1, 39.2, 39.2, 39.3, 39.3, 39.4, 39.4, 39.5, 39.6, 39.7, 39.7, 39.8, 39.8, 39.9, 39.10, 39.10, 39.11, 39.11, 39.12, 39.12, 39.13, 39.13, 39.14, 39.15, 39.15, 39.16, 39.16, 39.17, 39.17, 39.18, 39.19, 39.20, 39.20, 39.21, 39.21, 39.22, 39.22, 39.23, 39.23, 39.24, 39.25, 39.25, 39.26, 39.26, 39.27, 39.27, 39.28, 39.29, 39.29, 39.30, 39.30, 39.31, 39.31, 39.32, 39.32, 39.33, 39.33, 39.34, 39.34, 39.35, 39.36, 39.37, 39.37, 39.38, 39.38, 39.39, 39.39, 39.40, 39.40, 39.41, 39.42, 40.2, 41.1, 43.1, 43.1, 43.2, 43.3, 43.4, 43.4, 43.5, 43.5, 43.6, 43.7, 43.8, 43.8, 47.1, 47.2, 47.3, 47.4, 47.5, 52.1, 56.2, 56.4, 60.9, 60.10, 61.2, 61.4, 61.6, 64.11, 64.12, 64.13, 64.14, 64.15, 64.16, 64.17, 64.18, 64.19, 64.20, 66.1, 66.2, 66.4, 66.6, 66.8, 70.1, 70.2, 74.1, 74.2, 74.3, 74.4, 74.5, 74.6, 74.7, 74.8, 74.9, 74.10, 74.11, 74.12, 74.13, 74.14, 74.15, 74.16, 75.1, 82.1, 82.1, 82.2, 82.2, 82.3, 82.3, 82.4, 82.4, 82.5, 82.5, 82.6, 82.6. |PantherMedia GmbH (panthermedia.net), München: eriklam 11.2, 18.1; ibphoto 20.3. |Shutterstock.com, New York: 9nong 65.6, 65.12; Africa Studio 35.12, 42.2, 60.4; Andonova, Jasmina 39.56; andy0man 20.1; Artgraphixel 9.5; chonlasub woravichan 11.5, 18.6; DavidTB 42.4; Dell 72.1; Denis Kuvaev 32.4; fm.stockers 9.1; Fotogroove 9.6; Gemenacom 60.2; Gowanlock, Tom 51.1; Grinvalds, Kaspars 65.1, 65.7; Gyavcin 39.54; iravgustin 32.5; IrinaK 11.4, 18.3; Jagodka 55.12; Karandaev, Evgeny 35.8; Krakenimages.com 42.1; Kulniz 42.6; LaMantarraya 55.10; Lemonsoup14 35.13; LN_PHOTO 60.5; Luxury_Studio 4.1, 4.1, 4.2, 4.2, 4.4, 4.4, 4.5, 4.5, 4.8, 4.8, 4.9, 4.9, 4.10, 4.10, 19.4; May, Lena 32.6; MintImages 12.1; Miss Ty 42.5; Monkey Business Images 37.2, 37.7; nortongo 17.3; Obs70 71.1; Pahham, Pete 39.48; Panuwach 73.1, 73.1, 73.2, 73.2, 73.3, 73.3, 73.4, 73.4, 73.5, 78.3, 78.3, 78.4, 78.4, 78.5, 78.5, 78.7, 78.7, 78.8, 78.8, 78.9, 78.9; PhotobyTawat 60.8; Pixel-Shot 54.4; RemarkEliza 55.1, 83.1, 83.1; Samuilovs, Aleksandrs 27.3; schab 39.53; Shadrin, Artem 20.5; Song_about_summer 20.2; Stuchelova, Kuttelvaserova 39.61; Studio Romantic 42.8; Syda Productions 7.1, 7.2, 8.2; Violart 13.1; Yansh, Ka 35.10. |stock.adobe.com, Dublin: absolutimages 11.6, 18.2; allocricetulus 11.3; aneduard 55.3, 83.3, 83.3; BrAt82 54.3; cynoclub 18.4; Daisy Daisy 78.11, 85.5, 85.5; Dario Titel; DMM Photography Art 39.43; fortyforks 55.2, 83.2, 83.2; FotoJagodka 18.5; Gelpi 39.51, 39.52; HLPhoto 35.7; ink drop Titel; Jozsef, Szasz-Fabian 39.44; kite_rin 37.6; Kostic, Dusan 37.3; Krakenimages.com 55.5, 83.5, 83.5; Kurhan 39.55, 60.1; LIGHTFIELD STUDIOS 28.2; Lund, Jacob 78.10, 85.4, 85.4; magmarcz 55.9; Monkey Business 55.4, 79.3, 83.4, 83.4; nadianb 54.1; New Africa 27.1, 31.10, 65.5, 65.11; PeJo 31.5; Pixel-Shot 20.6, 65.3, 65.9; pixelliebe 35.3, 45.1, 45.2, 45.2, 45.3, 45.3, 45.4, 45.4, 45.5, 45.5, 45.6, 45.6, 45.7, 45.7, 45.8, 45.8, 45.9, 45.9, 45.10, 45.10, 45.11, 45.11, 45.12, 45.12, 45.13, 45.13, 45.14, 45.14, 45.15, 45.15, 45.16, 45.16, 45.17, 45.17, 45.18, 45.18, 45.19, 45.19, 45.20, 45.20, 45.21, 45.21, 45.22, 45.22, 45.23, 45.23, 45.24, 45.24, 45.25, 45.25, 45.26, 45.26, 45.27, 45.27, 45.28, 45.28, 45.29, 45.29, 45.30, 45.30, 45.31, 45.31, 45.32, 45.32, 45.33, 45.33, 45.34, 45.34, 45.35, 45.35, 45.36, 45.36, 45.37, 45.37, 64.1, 64.2, 64.3, 64.4, 64.5, 64.6, 64.7, 64.8, 64.9, 64.10; pololia 19.1; Ranta Images 39.47; Ternavskaja, Olga 39.50; Tim UR 27.5; victoria p. 54.2; Voronin, Vladimir 76.1, 76.2; Wodicka, Erwin 79.2; Wylezich, Björn 20.4; ©Andrey Popov 60.6.